# TARI ®
# THE KEY TO HIDDEN PROFIT

*Actual Case Histories of 21 Businesses*

*by*

KEITH N. CLELAND PHD, FCPA

Copyright © 2013 Keith N. Cleland PhD, FCPA

All rights reserved.

ISBN-10: 148120582X

EAN-13: 9781481205825

# TARI ®
# THE KEY TO HIDDEN PROFIT

*Actual Case Histories of 21 Businesses*

*by*
KEITH N. CLELAND PHD, FCPA

# TABLE OF CONTENTS

| | |
|---|---|
| Acknowledgements | vii |
| Foreword | ix |
| Introduction | xiii |
| List of Case Studies | xix |
| Comments by Managers | 127 |
| Comments by Accountants | 135 |
| About the Author | 143 |
| Definition of Terms | 147 |
| Fast Track Problem Resolution Guide | 149 |
| Epilogue | 151 |
| Appendix | 155 |

# ACKNOWLEDGEMENTS

*Without Carolyn's love and prayerful support along with Paul and Suzy's belief that TARI® is 'awesome', it is unlikely this book would have been written...*

---

*A grain of sand can achieve little or nothing by itself, but in conjunction with many grains can be used to build dam walls, erect houses and construct highways; so it is with ideas like* TARI®. *Without the active support of members of the accounting profession concerned to do more for their clients, it would have remained just an idea. I acknowledge in particular -*

*The original group of 17 who came together in February 1980 at St John's College, University of Queensland, and who opened up their practices to permit access to their clients.*

*David Hartley, developer of the world's first professional accounting system, who made it possible for me to address those accountants from which the original group was selected and who has continued to provide assistance over the years. Several hundred partners of accounting practices in Australia, South Africa and the UK, who willingly gave time and energy to actively introduce TARI® to their client base.*

*My computer partner Trevor Watters, member of the original group, accountant turned software guru whose unique skills made the development of TARI® software available initially for the accounting profession and subsequently for the business end user.*

*Owners and managers of businesses, small and large, who have participated and enjoyed the benefits of TARI® firsthand.*

*On behalf of myself and the unnumbered businesses that will find new strength, direction and purpose from applying TARI®, I salute you all.*

# FOREWORD

*Ronen Day is the Managing Director of Fine Tubes Ltd. He has spent most of his career successfully improving business performance at a senior management level in industry and with PA Consulting Group, a leading International Management Consultancy. He is a Chartered Engineer with a Masters in Business Administration from London Business School.*

I first met Keith when he was delivering a seminar on his approach to improving business performance, which is the subject of this book. I was interested by his claim that you could manage a business by focusing on two key levers, which if correctly identified, could help you steer a business to growth and prosperity.

I had by that time been instrumental in improving the performance of many blue chip companies while working for a leading international business consultancy group. As a result, it seemed clear to me that improving business performance was not entirely straight forward and required the knowledge and experience of the complete range of functional and process management disciplines, which I had acquired over the years.

I found his concepts interesting but like many people who are first introduced to this approach did not really grasp the underlying principles and so concluded it was too simplistic to have any meaningful application in my world of business (where I believed the problems were much more complex and thereby required more sophisticated solutions).

It was about a year later that our paths crossed again while he was working in the UK applying his ideas. He persuaded me that if you could create the right focus in business, develop an expectation of success and create a simple plan that linked activity to financials, this would in itself deliver significant improvement in profitability. I agreed to trial his concepts on the business I was currently consulting, even though I was incredulous of his claims of the scale of improvement this could deliver.

Over the next few weeks I was constantly punctuated by Keith who would say: "Just trust me and follow the process and you will see the profit improvement you seek." This was an act of faith, as this process was so different from the well-established approaches to business improvement that had delivered so much success for my colleagues and me.

What I experienced was a revelation, as the owner with low aspirations and a lack of direction saw his business transformed in less than a year into a dynamic business with a growth in profitability which I would only expect to see in a Disney movie. I became a firm believer in Keith's concepts but incredulous it had taken me so long to grasp such an obvious truth. Even then I was not convinced the concepts would work in larger organizations.

Sometime later I was consulting with a much larger business which was losing money and ridden with debt. There were many issues that we were working on that needed to be resolved. One evening over a glass of wine with Keith discussing various business issues, he suggested I apply his concepts to this company. I was skeptical whether we would get much benefit for the effort we would need to invest in this larger and more sophisticated organization, although I could see merit in doing some product analysis.

The journey that followed was different from what I had expected. What I had not realized was that the ability of the various departmental managers to contribute was being clouded by their functional performance measures and the opaqueness of costing and financial systems. (This was not the first time I had come across senior business managers who could not relate the profits on financial statement to their own activities). What was more, the people who worked at all levels down to the shop floor, wanted the company to survive, but did not have the focus or understanding of how they could contribute to making the company a success.

## Foreword

Keith's concepts provided the company with this much needed focus and empowered the organization very quickly. Sales and production worked on business activity levels; designers redesigned product with marketing using the added value per hour concept; sales became much more effective in managing product margins; shop floor operators could directly relate their efforts to the company's profitability and managers had a simple and understandable way of driving the business forward that related their efforts to the profitability of the business. In three years the debts were cleared and the company was making healthy operating profits.

I believe Keith's work, will one day be regarded as a landmark contribution to business owners and managers around the world. I encourage you to read this book and hope that you will find the success that I have found by applying Keith's concepts to your organization.

**Ronen Day**
*September 2008*

# INTRODUCTION

TARI® stands for Target Average Rate Index, the application of which will become clear in the Case Studies. Originally referred to as Contribution Based Activity, the term evolved out of my consulting work with business clients of public accountants.

It had all started when a printer asked me if I could help him. It appeared he put 25% on every job but never made more than 5% at the end of a year. As a professor of management accounting with a consulting background, I thought it would provide an excellent case study for 3rd year students. Explained in Case Study 2, the successful outcome led in time, to TARI®.

In the early days of advising companies with the application of TARI®, although I knew the concept worked, I struggled to explain the underlying principle of why it worked so effectively. It was not until a year or so after Case Study 9 about the hard pressed diesel repair business, that I began to see the light.

Cases ranged from sole proprietorships to multinationals and size made little difference to the outcomes. At one stage I was invited to introduce the concept to the national partners and staff of a multinational accounting practice. Employing 200 partners and 1,200 staff, the firm was becoming increasingly alarmed at the leakage of clients to competitors charging lower fees. The assignment ran over a two-year period, giving me the chance to follow through the application of TARI® to 78 of several hundred larger clients audited by the firm.

Initial analysis showed that 6 of the 78 were well on the way to a possible liquidation and 23 were in negative profit and heading into difficulties. The stories of these businesses would be worthy of a book by themselves. I particularly recall one of them manufacturing plastic items: while the senior audit partner was congratulating the client on gaining a substantial order, I quietly calculated the 18 plastic-molding machines were working at 45% of capacity - or the equivalent of 3hrs 36 minutes per machine per 8 hour day.

On breaking the news to the client, he picked up the phone and dialed his brother in the factory. "Bill, can you come here immediately please!" Bill arrived dressed in grimy overalls face and arms smudged with grease and looking as though he had been up all night.

"Do you realise we are only 45% productive?" his brother shouted.

"It is it that much?" said Bill; "I've been trying to tell you for the past two years that if we don't start upgrading our machines, we won't be in business at all!"

As I visited one client after another in different parts of the country, the stories were of a similar ilk, as indeed, they would continue to be wherever one travelled.

"I can see that I am really in the business of selling time and product happens to be the output," exclaimed one proprietor following a pricing review of his product range. He was right. The review showed that although he paid for 20,000 hours of potential activity, only 10,000 or 50% could be traced to output. Quite clearly, the leakage was adversely affecting the bottom line.

Lying at the core of any business, small or large, retail or non-retail, time is inextricably linked to financial contribution. Financial statements providing historical feedback on financial contribution, with no indication or mention of physical output, be it man-hours or number of sales, are not unlike malfunctioning speedometers, revealing distance but no indication of speed.

In allocating and tracking costs on a variety of job or cost centers, management accounts while theoretically correct, tends to fragmentation rather than consolidation – numerous pages of computer printout providing management with anything but a

## Introduction

woods' view. The attempt to diagnose cost structures in business to determine the cost effectiveness of various parts, over-reached itself with Activity Based Costing – now discredited by its founders and revamped as an equally cost-focused and expensively complex 'Time Based ABC.'

In essence, a business needs to cover expenses and make a profit. Normally it does this by trying to achieve a sufficient margin between the sale price and the cost price of goods or materials. By frequent comparison of the margin per sale in conjunction with the number of sales, TARI® focuses attention on the connection between a sale and its impact on the bottom line, prompting for a more balanced and profitable performance. (See the 'Business Wheel' in Appendix)

The case studies illustrate the changes – often dramatic - that take place when management makes the connection between quote or price and the bottom line, demonstrating how the connection can be used to advantage across the spectrum of business, private or corporate, small or large, retail or non-retail.

Readers conversant with matters of finance and economics may wonder at first glance, whether this is much ado about nothing. If so, a cursory reading of one or two case studies will help focus their attention, particularly when they see that despite the availability of fully qualified professionals in both IT and accounting, that:

- if management of a manufacturing plant had analyzed just 2 or 3 invoices of a contract supplying 55% of output to a large customer, it would have alerted them to the impact of a potentially damaging blow to the business;
- if the retailer had understood the connection between input and output, he would readily have used the available point of sale information long before he finally got the message of how to turn his business around;
- if the large corporate with 400 subsidiaries and substantial accounting expertise, had grasped the connection between invoice and bottom line, it would not have sold a break-even subsidiary that went on to net a profit of $2.5m in the ensuing ten months prior to a successful float on the ASX.

Simple as the TARI® concept may be, experience over many years has shown its very simplicity can inhibit comprehension and obscure the dynamism of its impact. In particular, for those who specialize in financial and management accounting, the concepts often need time to sink in. One CA/CPA in particular comes to mind. He arranged a seminar at which I addressed about 100 of his clients. This was followed by a several days of interviews with clients wanting more information about the application to their businesses. A two-year period ensued, during which there was little if any communication before he suddenly appeared out of the blue shouting, "I've got it. Damn it, I've got it!"

Just why it has taken so long for the accounting profession to come to terms with the needs of its business clients has much to do with pressures to meet increasingly onerous demands by government and other statutory bodies. The same pressures however, are the prime source of fees supplying the needs of the great majority of accounting practices. In a regulatory environment, where the only measure of performance required is accuracy of income and expenditure, there has been no call for comparing actual output with potential output as a statutory requirement of financial statements, although such a disclosure would provide a significant first step towards improving productivity and bottom line performance underpinning a nation's economy.

This book has been written in the hope that businesses everywhere will 'get it' and in doing so relieve a sizable chunk of the stress that presses unceasingly from all sides.,Born out of the need to provide what really matters when quoting or pricing the TARI® benchmark arising out of the CBA concept, has been tested and applied at the coal-face of numerous businesses of all shapes and sizes. The real life case studies in the following pages clearly show that if focus can be sustained on the contribution per unit of the key driver, the rest tends to take care of itself.

Of the 21 businesses in the case studies, 18 were referred to the author by their external CA/CPA accountants. Realizing the gap in their professional education, these accountants and several hundred of their colleagues, cooperated in an active outreach to get the message to their clients by conducting seminars, workshop

## Introduction

and interviews over the past 2 decades. Without their input, it is unlikely the concept would have seen the light of day.

For those wishing to understand what the concept is all about, a reading of a few case studies will provide a far greater awareness than any additional explanation that could be contained within the confines of an introduction.

Because the concept applies universally to all business - from the corner store to the multinational, the case studies cover both small and large business. Either way, readers looking for value, will find nuggets of gold applicable to their business.

# LIST OF CASE STUDIES

| # | Case Study | Page |
|---|---|---|
| 1 | **Kitchen Utensil Manufacturer Taken to the Cleaners** *Following installation of new hardware and software, growing doubts about the viability of the business prompts the CEO to ask for help.* | 1 |
| 2 | **Printing Business Multiplies Net Profit by 500%** *Unable to see a connection between adding 25% profit to every job and ending up with 5%, the Printer is instrumental in giving birth to TARI®* | 7 |
| 3 | **Furniture Manufacturer Climbs Out of the Red** *6 months input by a leading consulting group fine-tuning production and marketing, failed to stem the slide, despite a new product sending the plant into overdrive.* | 15 |
| 4 | **Contractor Overcomes Competition to Make Profit** *Quoting at a price necessary to cover expenses and profit, a contractor finds he cannot win jobs and must reduce his price. But doing so means foregoing profit.* | 21 |
| 5 | **Horticultural Equipment Proprietor's Moment of Truth** *Struggling to repay the bank, the proprietor blamed himself for going into debt against his better instincts. But the debt was not the cause of his problem at all.* | 27 |

| | | |
|---|---|---|
| 6 | **Wholesaler Nets $2.5m in 10+ Months** | 35 |
| | *A management buy-out of a company being sold for lack of profitable performance, illustrates what can happen when targets are broken into digestible proportions.* | |
| 7 | **Jeweler's Changed Focus Turns Red into Black** | 41 |
| | *Dependent on passing tourist trade, this Jeweler found it impossible to do more than cover costs, let alone make a profit.* | |
| 8 | **Upmarket Café Learns How to Stay on Track** | 47 |
| | *Two friends in the hospitality industry open a café in an upmarket suburb and strike problems on the opening day. Fortunately, they had a wise mentor.* | |
| 9 | **Diesel Repair Shop Rescued from Sand-Up Hill Country** | 51 |
| | *A top sales engineer deciding on a change of lifestyle takes over a rural diesel repair business. As the business heads into liquidation, his wife discovers the way out.* | |
| 10 | **Garment Maker Multiplies Net Profit by 700%** | 57 |
| | *Caught up in the traditional approach to pricing, the CEO and Sales Manager are excited when they see the possibilities open up with the application of TARI®* | |
| 11 | **Switchboard Manufacturer Climbs into the Black** | 65 |
| | *While senior management held to conflicting views about the cause of declining profitability, a representative sample of invoices helped pinpoint the problem in minutes.* | |
| 12 | **Baker Identifies Where the Rubber Meets the Road** | 71 |
| | *Immersed in baking and distributing 750 products from meat pies to crumpets, it came as a shock when management caught a glimpse of the woods from down in the trees.* | |
| 13 | **Architectural Practice Eradicates Malignant Cancer** | 77 |
| | *A variety of hourly charge rates based on salary levels coupled with dysfunctional time sheets were creating a major distraction until the partners were shown a new way.* | |
| 14 | **Accounting Firm Wins by Losing a Third of Its Fees** | 83 |
| | *Losing a client to a departing staff member is an ever present concern for professional firms - a problem this particular practitioner succeeded in overcoming.* | |

## List of Case Studies

**15 Legal Firm Transfers Productivity to Bottom Line** — 89
*Uncovering a major roadblock to productivity spurred this legal practitioner into clearing the backlog of files strewn across the office floor.*

**16 Contractor Increases Strike Rate to 1 in 4** — 95
*A multinational air-conditioning group teaches its contractors across the world how to quote to win installations. This contractor quoted differently.*

**17 Hot Bread Baker Discovers More to Bread than Flour** — 99
*Until he came face-to-face with the added value in bread and sausage rolls, the proprietor was actively seeking additional products to boost the bottom line.*

**18 Window Manufacturer's Flawed Foundation** — 105
*The fabricator putting a window together was the most productive of all on the assembly floor. It wasn't his fault that the method of assembly was hopelessly inefficient.*

**19 Multi-Home Contractor Discovers a New Way Home** — 109
*From the design to the completed house, all looked good on paper, but slippage was occurring. Figuring a way to make the supervisors more accountable turned the situation around.*

**20 Hairdressing Salon Cuts Its Way Out of Closedown** — 115
*The national award 'Hairdresser of the Year' came at a time when the salon was in danger of closure. By chance, it was selected by a Reality TV Series seeking to film the impact of TARI®.*

**21 Multi-Department Store Whitewashes the Past** — 121
*It was hammered home that genius was 20% but implementation was 80% of the exercise. This assignment demonstrates a tried and tested technique that makes things happen.*

# CASE STUDY 1:

# KITCHEN UTENSIL MANUFACTURER TAKEN TO THE CLEANERS

**F**ollowing installation of new hardware and software, growing doubts about the viability of the business prompts the CEO to ask for help.

I had just finished speaking with a group of chief executive officers and was packing my computer and overhead projector prior to catching a taxi to the airport when Brian tapped me on the shoulder.

"Would you have time to speak with my accountant at my plant?" he asked.

The time was 11.30am. "I really need to be at the airport by 1230 to catch the 1pm flight to Sydney" I replied with a sympathetic smile.

"Well, the plant is on the way. If you could just spare 20 minutes I could get you to the airport in good time." There was such a sense of need in his tone that I agreed to go with him.

On the way he told me his plant manufactured kitchen utensils for nationwide distribution and that they had recently upgraded all information systems with new hardware and software at the cost of $500,000, primarily to improve overall control of production, pricing and inventory. Although the system was designed and installed by one of the Big Four accounting firms in whom he had complete trust, the information pouring out was so extensive he felt he had lost his grip on the business. That in conjunction with a slowing down of cash flow, told him things were not as they should be.

At the plant, I was ushered into a conference room where to my surprise, the accountant sat waiting together with the consultant responsible for design and installation of the software. To suggest the atmosphere was distinctly chilly would be an understatement.

I went straight to the whiteboard and asked the accountant to give me the planned gross profit for the year. He had no trouble locating the figure and I wrote it on the board.

I asked for the number of production hours planned for the same period. He quickly nominated an amount, which I wrote on the board and then divided the gross profit by the hours. The result came to $80.

"Would you agree the target average gross profit per production hour for the planned period is $80?" I asked the accountant.

Several seconds passed before he nodded agreement.

"I refer to the $80 as TARI®, short for target average rate index - probably the most important of all benchmarks."

"Never heard of it!" he snapped.

"What percentage of your output do you sell to your best customer?" I asked.

"Our best customer takes 55%" Brian, the CEO interjected beginning to wonder where all this was heading.

"Then can we access 3 or 4 typical invoices for this customer together with the cost of materials used and production hours?" I asked.

## Kitchen Utensil Manufacturer Taken to the Cleaners

While the accountant left the room to locate the invoices, the consultant broke the silence to drive home his credentials, pointing out that in addition to his role as a senior consultant with one of the 'Big Four' with extensive involvement with major companies in the region, he lectured on management accounting part-time at the university.

With three invoices to hand, it took less than 5 minutes to demonstrate that the average gross profit per production hour for this customer worked out at $33.

| Invoice No. | Inv Price net of tax $ A | Materials Used $ B | Gross Profit $ C = A - B | GP % D = C / A | Hours No. E | Ave per hour $ F = C / E |
|---|---|---|---|---|---|---|
| 2765 | 100,000 | 68,000 | 32,000 | 32 | 914 | 35 |
| 2958 | 300,000 | 200,000 | 100,000 | 33 | 3,125 | 32 |
| 3015 | 150,000 | 102,000 | 48,000 | 32 | 1,450 | 33 |
| Total | 550,000 | 370,000 | 180,000 | 33 | 5,489 | 33 |

I pointed out "you are getting an average gross profit of $33 per hour from a customer taking 55% of output, when you really need an average of $80!" There was dead silence.

"I really think it's time to get going to the airport." I said, placing the whiteboard marker back in its slot.

Reaching for his car keys on the table, Brian gave a loud sigh "I knew I was being screwed," he said, "I just didn't know how much!"

As we left the room, the eyes of both the accountant and the consultant were fixed on the whiteboard, struggling to come to terms with the findings.

"They threatened to take their business offshore," said Brian, referring to his best customer as we drove off. "I knew something was wrong but couldn't put my finger on it. Guess I allowed myself to be persuaded by all the calculations the accountant came up with about the deal making a marginal contribution."

> As the flight took off, I leaned back in my seat thinking of Brian and the half million he had spent installing hardware and software to get control of his business, only to find he was unable to see the wood for the trees. More to the point, the installation failed to provide the key information that he needed when making decisions vital to the future viability of the company.
>
> I wondered why should it be so difficult to identify the best customer is contributing $33 an hour compared with a TARI® of $80.
>
> Could the customer have contracted to take products from the lower price range of output to which lower markups applied and that the invoices failed to represent a typical range of low and high priced products? Given the reputation the buyer enjoyed as a distributor of quality products, it was more likely the price had been driven down to the bone.
>
> The fact is that none of the numerous businesses I had introduced to TARI® had analyzed one or more invoices to highlight gross profit per unit along the lines demonstrated. In this case, the hourly rates were fairly consistent, but in most cases, the rates varied significantly.
>
> Accounting theory, which drives commercial software, tends to focus on the nitty-gritty at the expense of the big picture – obscuring the real day-to-day decision-making needs of management and supervisors. A cornerstone of the accounting profession proclaims the need for information to be timely and relevant. In Brian's as with 95% of businesses, the feedback was neither timely nor relevant.

In theory, jobs costed and quoted, product mix agreed and contracts signed are based on distributing all relevant costs, overheads, and profit, according to an assumed level of key activity - such as productive hours in non-retail and number of sales in retail. However, the actual level of output activity is never identified as such in typical financial statements and only in retrospect in management accounts, fragmented into variances of one type or another.

The reality is that summary data arriving two to three weeks into the following month bears little relevance to jobs costed and sales made a few weeks earlier.

It seems no theory other than that referred to as TARI®, stresses the need to provide a benchmark against which the gross profit contribution of output activity can be compared on an invoice-by-invoice basis.

The following real-life case history of a Printing business highlights the problem of identifying the levels of output activity – normally referred to as productivity.

It happens to be the Printer who sparked my original involvement with the concepts underlying TARI®.

CASE STUDY 2:

# PRINTING BUSINESS MULTIPLIES NET PROFIT BY 500%

**U**nable to see a connection between adding 25% profit to every job and ending up with 5%, the Printer is instrumental in giving birth to TARI®

"I don't understand it at all: I put twenty five percent profit on every job and never get more than five percent by the end of the year. What am I doing wrong?" asked the Printer.

"I don't know," I replied, "but we can soon find out." After twelve years as a professor of Accounting and Business Studies, specializing in management accounting, I was yet to learn how to pinpoint the cause of such problems without extensive time-consuming analysis. Nevertheless, I was confident we would find the solution.

Seeing the exercise as a potential hands-on challenge for final year students, I sent three of them to the printing firm to collect a sample of jobs for analysis. When they came back with 3,000 job envelopes selected at random from the past three years, I was not entirely unhappy to note the task would last for several tutorials.

Eventually the analysis was completed. "He puts an average of twenty five percent profit on every job" they reported, "and ends up with five percent."

"So what's the conclusion?" I asked.

"Well, he's right," they answered with a smile.

It occurred to me that their somewhat circular conclusion was doing no more than reflecting the outcome of three years of conventional accounting studies.

Sensing the problem was connected with too many gaps between jobs, and lacking any other information, we decided to check the times the printing machines operated. Gaining the co-operation of very skeptical employees, we ran the check for five days to find the six printing machines operated for less than two hours each out of an eight-hour day.

In the face of the printer's refusal to accept the findings, we ran the check for another week with much the same result.

While the time check was underway, I spent time observing the routine. It went something like this: a customer would ask for 10,000 letterheads "the same as last time." The work envelope for the previous occasion was located and a new job card inserted. The foreman looked at the job and wrote down the estimated times for compositing, printing, and binding. The job card was forwarded in the envelope to the person graced with the description of Cost Accountant. He in turn reached for a plastic covered sheet containing the costing for every category of work, and taking account of the foreman's times, jotted down the costs in pencil.

At the completion of the job, the Printer took the work envelope home along with fifty or so other envelopes in order to finalize the pricing over a weekend. This process involved reviewing the proposed price and making such adjustments as he considered relevant and in line with what may have been charged previously or how much could be added - or deleted - according to his best knowledge of the client and his 'feelings' for an appropriate fit.

I recall being mildly shocked to realize the exact, if not exacting, science of cost accounting occupying a significant portion of the undergraduate degree, had but passing relevance to the realities of pricing in practice.

The Printing and Allied Trades Manual for members set out the complete rationale of costing and pricing precisely as would be found in any management accounting textbook. Nevertheless, having established the various costs according to theory, the matter appeared to terminate at that point. Each job was seen to be contributing to profit but in absence of tracking the total time taken by jobs completed and billed, the theory broke down. Monthly profit and loss and balance sheet financial statements did not refer to gaps between jobs.

Driven to find cash to meet the weekly wage bill and satisfy demanding suppliers as well as an anxious bank manager, the Printer targeted cash, not profit, and for all practical purposes treated the two as identical. Cash in the bank meant wages and anxious suppliers could be paid without too much stress.

"As I see it," I said to the Printer, following several weeks of reviewing the whole process of theory and practice, "excluding paper, ink, negatives and out-sourced work, you need to cover $350,000 expenses for the year and if you add a further $100,000 to cover net profit, you need a gross profit of $450,000." In view of a record profit of $35,000 achieved five years earlier, his look of disbelief at the $100,000 profit was palpable.

I pressed on, "You have ten staff engaged in hands-on production with 1,800 hours each available for charging, or 18,000 hours in total. Assuming 50% of those hours can be charged to jobs - bearing in mind last year was a lot less according to the checks we made - then we have 9,000 hours to achieve $450,000, or an average of $50 an hour."

He threw up his hands. "Our hourly charge rates are $20. We'd go out of business in a month."

I picked up an invoice for $900 lying on his desk. "What was the cost of materials used in this job?" I asked.

He seemed to know the answer without referring to the work envelope. "$300" he said.

"How many hours did you estimate the job would take when you quoted?"

"10 hours."

I deducted $300 from the $900 and divided the resulting gross profit of $600 by 10 hours.

"Well that works out at $60 an hour."

He stared in disbelief. "How come?" he asked.

"Well, when you apply markup to materials and markup to labor to cover overheads and a further 25% to cover profit plus a little extra to cover 'feelings' and so forth, you get $60 an hour."

"But that includes profit and markup and everything."

"That's right, and that's what the overall target average gross profit rate of $50 includes.[1] The key is to make sure you get the target chargeable hours of 9,000 a year, or an average of 200 hours a week for a 45 week year."[2]

He shook his head slowly, intrigued yet mystified.

"Let's run it alongside the existing system for a month or two," I suggested, "we can't go too far off track." I was even more tentative than the Printer, wondering if my efforts at simplification had missed something important. The thought of running it as a trial appealed to me as much as to him.

We met every week and checked progress by simply listing quotes for the week, deducting the materials from the sale price, and dividing by the quoted or estimated hours. If the gross profit contribution of a quote came in at less than $50, he would review ways and means to do the job in less time in order to get closer to or exceed the $50.

Billings were tracked weekly and accumulatively to compare hours and contribution with the average weekly target of 200 hours x $50.

---

[1] To emphasize its benchmark status and avoid confusion with a 'cost' target average rate became known as Target Average Rate Index or TARI®

[2] 52 weeks less 7 weeks - (4 weeks annual holiday + 10 days public holiday + 5 days sick leave).

# Printing Business Multiplies Net Profit by 500%

As his confidence increased, he began to target jobs showing a higher contribution than $50 as well as fine-tuning the hours of jobs with lower contribution.

It was this step-by-step, quote-by-quote, job-by-job decision-making at the coalface that began to make the difference.

After 10 weeks the hours charged to jobs totaled 1,800 hours, or 200 hours below the 2,000-hour target; but the gross profit contribution rate was averaging $60 an hour or $10 above the $50 TARI® benchmark. The business was running $8,000 ahead of targeted net profit.

Encouraged we pressed on and after 20 weeks found that chargeable hours of 3600 were 400 hours below target but the average hourly rate had escalated to $65, or $15 above the target average rate of $50. In all, the firm was $34,000 ahead of targeted net profit.

|  | Total Weeks A | Total Hours B | Ave $GP per hour C | Total $GP D = (B x C) | Difference $ |
|---|---|---|---|---|---|
| Target | 10 | 2000 | $50 (TARI®) | $100,000 |  |
| Actual | 10 | 1800 | $60 | $108,000 | +$8000 |
| Target | 20 | 4000 | $50 (TARI®) | $200,000 |  |
| Actual | 20 | 3600 | $65 | $234,000 | +$34,000 |

Being well ahead of target, we discussed the possibility of getting his foot in the door of one or two larger companies and quote for long-run jobs that could keep the machines running in the down times. With his growing awareness of where the bottom line was at, he was in a position to under quote any competitor if he wished and still makes a contribution to the net profit providing he left some margin on materials.

He started with a major mining group and went on to secure several long-term contracts from major companies.

In time, following his election as State President of the Printing and Allied Trades, he was nominated to chair the National Conference for Printers. I suggested it might be a good idea to prepare a joint paper on what had obviously proved to be a significant breakthrough for presentation to the participants.

"Great idea," he said, "In fact I did think about asking you to speak. But on second thoughts decided it could wait until I retire."

> The owner of a printing firm with $12 million turnover wondered what relevance the story of this small printer had for his much larger business. I explained that just as the principle of gravity applies regardless of size, so it is with TARI®. It is universally applicable regardless of size.
>
> Like the printer, a business may have planned for a level of sales and profit but only finds out along the way, usually as cash flow falters, that the plan has fallen by the wayside. The case history of the printer highlights a key problem facing business in general, retail and non-retail, large and small, chasing sales based on the traditional approach to pricing jobs or products and overlooking the basis upon which that pricing is established i.e., the level of chargeable or output activity.
>
> For example, if costs + profit of $450,000 are allocated to a planned 15,000 units of output activity which fades over time to 9,000 units, then the required contribution will rise from $30 to $50 per unit. Obviously pricing on the basis of 15,000 units would be heading for trouble.
>
> If the actual level of output activity is not considered when preparing a quote or invoice, the connection between the invoice and bottom line remains in limbo.
>
> Normally, weekly and accumulative feedback will be enough to sustain the connection.

# Printing Business Multiplies Net Profit by 500%

The $50 TARI® is based on achieving $450,000 from 9,000 hours of chargeable output. It acts as a benchmark, prompting for action if a job shows a lesser contribution. Together with the targeted units of activity – in this case an average of 200 hours per week – it provides a direction against which overall l performance can be tracked and corrected as required.

In summary, whatever method is adopted when costing or pricing, at the end of the day, after paying trade suppliers for goods and materials, a business must cover its costs and make enough profit to sustain working capital, if it is to survive and grow. The total of costs + profit can be broken down into manageable daily or weekly gross profit targets. Of the numerous activities taking place at any one time, there is a key activity fundamental to and driving the rest. In the case of the Printer, the key activity underpinning output is man-hours. By dividing the overall target gross profit (costs + profit) by the number of man-hours we expect to charge to output, we get an average gross profit per man-hour referred to as TARI® or Target Average Rate Index. "Index" is used to emphasize its benchmark status and distinguish it from a cost.

Now we are in a position to compare each quote, job, or sale with a benchmark that reflects the requirements of our business and will help keep us on track.

TARI® can be used to advantage in several ways. One of which will be explored in the following case history.

## CASE STUDY 3:

# FURNITURE MANUFACTURER CLIMBS OUT OF THE RED

**6** months of fine-tuning by a leading consulting group, failed to stem the slide, despite a new product sending the plant into overdrive.

While in the UK, I contacted an old friend, Peter, who was working as a senior consultant with a widely respected international consulting group. He was currently applying his skills to a major furniture manufacturer on the outskirts of London.

He said he had been on the assignment for the past six months, focusing on improving throughput in the factory and achieving a measure of success. He had recently turned his attention to streamlining marketing procedures, getting the sales representatives to reassess the value of their calls and looking at ways and means of

## TARI ® The Key to Hidden Profit

establishing a more effective promotional campaign. Even so, he admitted he had been unable to stem the downward slide in the bottom line.

Knowing he had a grasp of TARI® concepts, I queried whether he was using them on the assignment. He said that his client employed over 750 of whom 26 were in the accounting office and 21 in IT, all highly qualified and providing up-to-date feedback from state of the art software. Given the exponential changes that had taken place in production due to robotic machinery, he considered man-hours in production was of minimal consequence in matters of costing and pricing, and that TARI® appeared to him to be focused on man-hours as the key activity driver.

I reminded him that the key activity in any business large or small could vary from business to business and department to department within a business. It may be man or machine hours or square meters of partitioning, or cans of beans or tonnes per kilometer in non-retail sectors, or the number of sales measured by cash register check-out or invoice in retailing, meals served in a restaurant, bed-nights in a hospital, room nights in a motel and so forth.

For the sake of friendship if nothing else, he agreed to carry out a preliminary product analysis along TARI® lines, but without mentioning it to his client at the risk of losing face.

As it turned out, despite the extensive use of robotic equipment for cutting, turning and finishing, the costing was clearly based on man-hours as the common denominator. It was a simple matter to divide the overall planned gross profit by the planned man-hours - identified as 70% of available hours – to arrive at a TARI®[3] of £57.

From there it became a simple matter of comparing the actual gross profit per hour of each of the 120 products with the TARI® of £57.

Programmed to provide feedback in the traditional format, the existing software was unable to deliver, so Peter persuaded the

---

3   The planned or targeted average gross profit per unit is in effect a benchmark and referred to as target average rate index - TARI®. 'Index' is used to avoid confusion with it being treated as a rate to be quoted or applied.

IT department to write a program to extract the required information. It took 3 days and occupied a system analyst and two programmers to pinpoint the gross profit contribution per man-hour of each of the 120 products.

"I must say what surprises me is the range of contributions per man-hour. I would have expected a much greater consistency than is shown here," said Peter pointing to contributions ranging from £93 to £22. "I assumed the 50% mark-up on factory cost to cover overheads and profit would have resulted in a more even pattern of hourly rates." Yet only 19 of the 120 products contributed more than £57 per man-hour.

"The interesting thing about the products contributing more than £57 is that at least 4 are discontinued lines." He pointed to a product contributing £93 and another contributing £70. It was then his eyes settled on a product contributing £36 per hour. "Well I'm damned!" he exclaimed. "This is the product they are all excited about. It's selling into Europe like hotcakes and pushing production into overtime!"

He jumped up from his chair "There's obviously been a change in product mix and it hasn't been picked up!"

"What are you going to do about it?" I asked.

"Take it in and let them see it," he replied stuffing the papers in his brief case in a hurried exit to his car.

When we spoke a week or so later I asked about progress.

"The Finance Director wants to install the software. He was a bit defensive until he saw the Managing Director was not going to ask why it had not been picked up earlier. Now he is excited and wants to get with it. He says he had something similar in mind a year ago but didn't follow through."

"And the MD?" I asked.

"A bit early yet. He needs time to let it sink in. He has been working here since he was a boy on the production side and leaves all the figuring to the FD. Right now, we are checking the gross profit contribution to flow from the products planned for next year."

Another week passed before we met again to discuss progress.

"It would have been a disaster," Peter said. "As I mentioned, we had planned sales by multiplying out the sale price of each

## TARI ® The Key to Hidden Profit

product by the number we estimated we would sell and merely applied the estimated gross profit margin based on our 50% mark-up to arrive at the gross profit contribution. When we reworked the exercise using the TARI® approach, the e margin worked out far less than our estimates and that knocked the net profit for six."

By now, the MD had grasped the concept completely and was refusing to approve product designs that delivered a gross profit of less than £57 a man-hour. They were sent back for redesign. He organized a brainstorming session to work out how to reduce production time and cut the price of materials of products contributing less than £57 without affecting quality or changing the basic design. The exercise proved effective with the contribution from the best-selling product rising from £36 to £48 per man-hour.

The man-hours and the gross profit contribution contained in products invoiced were tracked weekly and accumulatively against plan. After eight weeks, the MD considered he finally had a grip on the business. So much so, walking around the factory one Friday afternoon and noting the hours being used to clean up before the employees knocked off - an event that had gone on for as many years as he could recall - he went back to his office and multiplied the hours by £57. Peter told me he found him with head in hands late that Friday evening having discovered the clean-up process was depleting the bottom line to the tune of £2 million a year.

In the belief that in-house labor was cheaper than outsourcing, he had consistently turned down offers by contractors to do all the cleaning for less than £150,000. However, his previous calculation of in-house v outsourcing costs was based on an in-house cost of £14 an hour, not £57.

Before I left the UK, some 3 months later, the bottom line had ceased its downward slide and was curving back into profit. Peter was asked to extend his assignment for a further 6 months.

# Furniture Manufacturer Climbs Out of the Red

One can only feel for the MD in such a situation, surrounded as he was by professionally well qualified Finance and IT departments including an FD upon whom he relied completely. His background and focus from the time he started with the business as a boy of 15 was production. It is not surprising he took several days to understand the essence of the matter, only to realize that both the diagnosis and the prescription for resolving the problem was so simple.

It was not as though he lacked information about the business. Along with all directors he received a 150 page monthly Board Pack covering every aspect of the business including a detailed list of where performance varied from target. If anything, he suffered from information overload.

Awareness of the direct relationship between the target gross profit and the man-hour gave him a grip on the business that he had never previously enjoyed.

Whereas the printer in the previous case study was unaware that he was getting close to 2 hours output for 8 hours pay, in this case, the output was known to be close to 75% or 6 hours per 8 hour day.

Even so, no connection had been made between the actual gross profit of a product and the overall targeted gross profit.

Assuming the costing had been carried out in line with the costing of all products, how could it happen that a product so much in demand returned such a low gross profit per man-hour of input?

It could be the time to make and assemble had been miscalculated, or the price of materials had risen without being noticed, leaving less margin available to cover expenses + profit.

It could also mean that retailer resistance or competition in the market place had caused a price cut or involved discounting.

The point is that none of these possibilities was detected in the midst of a myriad of numerous other activities taking place at the same time, and it was only the fortuitous intervention of TARI® that restored focus to what really mattered.

The following case study illustrates the interaction between output activity and gross profit per unit of that activity

## CASE STUDY 4:

# CONTRACTOR OVERCOMES COMPETITION TO MAKE PROFIT

Quoting at a price necessary to cover expenses and profit, a contractor finds he cannot win jobs and must reduce his price. However, doing so means foregoing profit.

He was one of ten interviewed following a seminar at which I had spoken on "How to Detect and Eradicate Malignant Cancer in Your Business" and had been intrigued by the thought of week by week tracking of charged time and wanted to discuss it further.

As an electrical contractor, he employed 20 technicians installing electrical circuits in high- rise buildings and had struggled to make profit during the past year.

Following a brief review of his situation, we projected a gross profit target by adding the anticipated expenses of the business to a healthy net profit for the year ahead.

Dividing the resulting gross profit by an estimated number of chargeable hours gave a target average gross profit per hour or TARI®, of $46. This was based on charging out 6 hours a day, 5 days a week and 45 weeks of the year.

In essence, to achieve his target for the year he would need to track an average of 600 hours a week (20 technicians x 30 hours each) for 45 weeks at an average contribution of $46 an hour.

Reviewing progress back in the accountant's office six months later, the contractor looked worried. "It's too competitive" he said, "I can't win quotes at $46 an hour and my order book is down to three weeks work at most."

"What can you win quotes for?" I asked

"$40."

I looked at him intently. To drop his TARI® from $46 to $40 would negate most, if not all his profit. I mentally reviewed the two levers: output activity - or number of hours charged - and the $gross profit rate per hour. If the $gross profit could not be achieved then output or productivity had to be increased. But in his case the tracking data indicated that he was achieving the targeted chargeable hours, which at 75% or six hours a day was maximum without going into overtime and thereby adding to the $gross profit rate.

For a moment, I experienced a fleeting sense of failure, with all its consequences for the contractor and the loss of face for his external accountant who had gone out on a limb to involve me with his clients. I recall standing there as the seconds ticked away, wondering what the solution could be.

To gain more time, I put out a feeler, "Are you achieving your quoted times or are you running over?"

"Some run over, some run under but on average they match up." he replied.

"Who does the quoting?" I asked

"The estimator." he replied

## Contractor Overcomes Competition to Make Profit

"How does he work out his times?"

"He has a pretty sophisticated software package that he works from."

"How does he work out times for the jobs then?"

"All the time sheets are fed to him. He records the times taken and uses them to update or develop times for all types of work."

"Does he carry out any work or method study of the jobs to check if they are being done efficiently or otherwise?"

He laughed at the thought "He hasn't been out of the office for the past five years to my knowledge; he's too flat out running his neck of the woods. No, he relies on the time sheets, and that is sensible enough. The men are fairly good with their times: we keep an eye on them."

"Do you remember me talking about human comfort level at the seminar?" I asked

"Yes I do, and I've thought about it," he replied.

"Where no plan or target or budget has been established, there is a tendency for effort to sink to human comfort level or HCL as I recall saying. If there has been no reassessment of times for jobs, the tendency will inevitably lean towards an expansion of those times. Imperceptible maybe, but inevitable." My confidence surged as I glimpsed a potential solution.

"What are you saying?"

"Well, if your estimator has been relying on time sheets to update times per job and using them in the quoting, those times will have blown out over the years. It is characteristic of time sheets."

"You mean we are over-quoting the time a job should take?"

"Exactly."

"Well what do we do? We don't have time to work or method-study the jobs. We would be out of business before we got started!"

I wrote $6 on the whiteboard and divided by $46 to get 13%.

"I suggest that for the moment, you get the estimator to take 13% off all times quoted and leave TARI® at $46. For example, if

23

you have job estimated to take 100 hours, cut the estimate to 87 hours."

"But why 13%?"

"Because that's the difference between $40 and $46 an hour. You believe you can win quotes at $40 an hour based on current estimator times. In that case, a job estimated at 100 hours by $40 brings in $4000. But you will also achieve $4000 if you target to complete the job in 13% less time i.e. 87 hours at $46 an hour."

I wrote on the whiteboard:

**100 hrs x $40       =       $4,000**

**87 hrs x $46        =       $4,002**

For a moment or two, he was nonplussed. "I don't know if we can do it. After all the men have a good idea of how a job should take."

"I'd be surprised if they track the times against the quote." I replied. "How much do they know about the quoted hours at the outset of a job?"

He shook his head, "I guess they don't. They just go to a job pretty much according to the schedule we put out at the beginning of each week."

"So if you want this to work for you, the men need to be aware of the targeted times."

"I guess that will lead to designing some sort of incentive system?" he queried with raised eyebrows.

"Whatever happens, don't even think of an incentive system until you bed down acceptance of completing a job in the targeted hours. And even then, any incentive should be based on what comes in over and above targeted net profit."

When speaking with the accountant six months later, he told me his client was on track to meet the targeted net profit.

# Contractor Overcomes Competition to Make Profit

The two keys of activity and gross profit contribution at the heart of every business are clearly demonstrated in this case study. If the desired gross profit rate is unachievable, the alternative is to review the level of chargeable or output activity.

If the level of chargeable activity cannot be achieved, the alternative is to review the gross profit rate, bearing in mind it is also possible to improve net profit by reducing the cost of materials or parts used as per the example below:

As an instrument for reviewing activity, time sheets are potentially useful but only if maintained accurately and compared with times quoted for a job. What really matters is what goes on between signing on and signing off.

Our research shows that time sheets are notoriously inaccurate as a guide to productivity and efficiency, and with few exceptions, times are seldom compared with times quoted.

Work-study covers the overall method as well as the timing of jobs. This case study is typical of businesses developed from a one-man start-up where the proprietor works for himself and awareness of what times a job should take is based primarily on his own input.

As the business grows and takes on more personnel, and the proprietor becomes increasingly distanced from the coalface, times inevitably blow out.

As the following real-life case study illustrates.

## CASE STUDY 5:

# HORTICULTURAL EQUIPMENT PROPRIETOR'S MOMENT OF TRUTH

Struggling to repay the bank, the proprietor blamed himself for going into debt against his better instincts. However, the debt was not the cause of his problem at all.

"I borrowed from the bank to buy a steel guillotine to save me taking my steel plate across town every time I wanted to get it cut, and now I can't pay make the repayments." Max was a man who hated the thought of borrowing because of the very problem he now found himself facing. The specter of potential disaster loomed large on his horizon.

He was making a variety of horticultural machines for polishing and packing fruit. The business had developed after he retired from a career in tool-making in order to purchase an avocado orchard. At the end of his first year on the orchard, when he came to wash, polish and pack the fruit he was unable to hire the necessary equipment or gain access to the local horticultural cooperative plant.

He bought steel, cut, welded, and mechanized his own plant. It was compact and highly efficient, so much so, demand for like models began to flow to the point where he built a large shed and hired labor. At the time of our meeting, the business was several years down the track, employing nine men in production with overseas exports well under way.

"Are your men busy?" I asked.

"Flat-out," he responded, giving an answer I had by now come to expect nine times out of ten.

"How do you know?" I pressed.

"They are good men. They like to live and work in the countryside; their children go to school here; their wives want to stay here. They don't belong to a union."

It not difficult to see why they liked living in the area: it was bathed with bright sunshine, refreshed by adequate rainfall, rich in volcanic soils that proliferated flowers, fruit, lush pastures and was minutes from endless miles of golden sands and rolling ocean surf.

"I can understand they like living here Max, but how do you know they are working productively?"

"What do you mean?"

"I mean, how do you know they are flat-out?"

"The window in my office looks over the factory and I can see them at work every time I look out." He omitted to mention he was away much of the time attending trade exhibitions, servicing customers and spearheading a thrust into overseas markets.

"Can we look at the output for the past year?" I asked, getting away from what threatened to be a talkfest to glance at the financial statements. They revealed no more than the conventional sales and expenses and made no reference to productivity.

In response to my request for something more helpful, he tabled a pile of thumb marked Invoice Books containing handwritten carbon copies of invoices.

# Horticultural Equipment Proprietor's Moment of Truth

We laboriously extracted each product sold, noting the cost of materials used and the estimated hours on a sheet of paper:

| Description | Units Sold | Man-hrs per Unit | Total Hours |
|---|---|---|---|
| Avocado | 30 | 60 | 1,800 |
| Nutcracker | 16 | 40 | 640 |
| Lychee Picker | 20 | 50 | 1,000 |
| Punnet Seeder | 14 | 80 | 1,120 |
| Total | 80 | 230 | 4,560 |

"You have nine in full-time production working how many hours?" I asked

"Forty hours a week each"

"Any overtime?"

"Yes, about four hours a week each. It gives them a bit of extra."

"That works out at roughly 2,000 hours per fulltime employee in production or 18,000 hours in all." I pointed out.

"Yes I see that" he said, "but so what?"

"Well, it means that you are paying 18,000 hours and only recovering 4,560 hours from output. That works out at close to 25% or two hours charged out per 8-hour day.

**Hours tracked in output:** 4,560

**Hours paid:** 18,000

**Productivity** $\frac{4,560}{18,000} \times 100$ = 25%

**25% x 8 hours** = **2 hours.**

29

**His chair fell backwards as he jumped up exclaiming**, "there must be more invoice books somewhere!" However, there were no more invoices. The invoice prices for the items listed added up to the year's sales spelt out in the financials.

"How is this possible?" he asked when he had settled down again. "None of them are slackers."

He picked up the financial statements, which compared last year with the previous year: "How come the sales have not dropped?" he asked with a tinge of doubt about the prognosis creeping into his voice.

"You mentioned you had put your prices up and the high returns flowing from the new punnet seeder have been masking productivity. The combination of falling output and increased expenses has put pressure on your ability to repay the loan."

"I don't understand it," he reiterated.

"It's fairly normal I assure you. You got things started; you worked out the times for each type of unit produced and you priced the jobs accordingly. The business grew and you found yourself attending trade shows and exhibitions, installing the units on properties, servicing the breakdowns, hiring new staff, interviewing sales reps, collecting the debts and paying the bills and spending many hours on new developments. Regardless of how hard you tried, you lost touch with the production throughput.

"And it's not that the men are slacking either. They are pacing themselves. Maybe the job that can be done in ten minutes is now done in twenty or more. You look around and they are all busy, but they have slowed down, knowing they will run out of work by the end of the day or week. Bring the work in and they'll speed up."

"How is it that my accountant doesn't tell me these things? He told me if he gives me regular figures, I could not go wrong. Now I see the position is serious even though sales are up on last year. What use are these figures to me?" He threw the statements into the waste bin.

"I'm sorry to have to say it Max, but if there is a textbook written that teaches how to identify levels of output or productive

## Horticultural Equipment Proprietor's Moment of Truth

activity and relate it to a financial contribution in a practical sense, the accounting profession hasn't advertised it. Current financial statements are not geared to pointing out that your production team achieved two hours output for eight hours pay.

"Quarterly statements such as you are getting are more helpful than annual statements, but they arrive a month after the period to which they refer, and the management information they provide is extremely limited. In any event, by the time they arrive it is a bit late to remedy what has already occurred. That's why you need to track progress weekly so as to be in a position to make corrections before problems bed down into the fabric."

"How would I get them weekly?" he asked, "The accountant's on my back enough as it is to get information every three months."

"Collecting the information necessary to give you the focus you need is not difficult. All you need so is complete a summary sheet of invoices once a week. After all, you only have one, two, or three invoices at the most to make out. You note the invoice number of the sale, the sale price, the cost price of materials, and the hours you quoted or established for the unit or units sold. You make sure it is filled in every Friday and add the total onto the previous totals so you keep a running check.

I sketched out a format to give him the idea:

| Invoice No. | Inv Price net of tax $ A | Materials Used $ B | Gross Profit $ C = A - B | GP % D = C / A | Hours E | Av GP per hr $ F = C / E | Target av GP per hr (TARI®) |
|---|---|---|---|---|---|---|---|
| 132 | 5,000 | 2,000 | 3,000 | 60 | 20 | 150 | |
| 138 | 12,000 | 6,000 | 6,000 | 50 | 50 | 120 | |
| 145 | 9,000 | 4,000 | 5,000 | 56 | 37 | 135 | |
| Total | 26,000 | 12,000 | 14,000 | 54 | 107 | 131 | |

"But I've got orders that take several weeks to put together."

"That's no problem. You only note the sales made. Work in progress is going on all the time and eventually translates into sales."

"What about the time spent on research and development of new machines and so on?"

"Do you use the production team to help you?"

"No, not really. Might use the foreman occasionally. I usually wait until they have knocked off for the day before I get down to it."

I suggested we look ahead and project likely expenses for next year. We worked our way down the list using his guesstimates. Excluding the cost of materials and out-sourced work, we totaled expense at $630,000.

"What shall we project for profit bearing in mind you broke even and covered expenses on 4,500 hours charged out? Just think of the potential if you can charge out 9,000 hours, which is still only 50% of the available 18,000 hours!"

The thought seemed to cheer him up and we targeted $270,000 net profit to arrive at a gross profit target of $900,000. We divided this by the targeted 9,000 chargeable hours to get a target average gross profit per hour of $100.

"Assuming a 45 week year and a target of 9,000 chargeable hours, you need 200 hours per week charged into product at an average gross contribution of $100 an hour. We refer to that average as the target average rate index or TARI®, so it will not be confused with a cost or a price. It is a benchmark against which you can compare the gross profit contribution per hour from any product or job."

I wrote the weekly target in the Action Sheet and summarized the key points of our discussion. *(See Case Study 21 for more on Action Sheets.)*

8 years passed and apart from an occasional phone call, we lost touch. That was before Max's wife rang to ask for help. She said profit had steadily increased over the years to $400,000 but that had fallen away to a loss of $150,000 during the past year. It seemed that when Max had semi retired and handed control to a newly appointed general manager, the business began to decline and they had reached the point where Max had to borrow heavily

## Horticultural Equipment Proprietor's Moment of Truth

against the security of their house and property to pay major creditors who would only supply materials for cash.

It did not take long to find out that comparison of invoices with TARI® along with weekly feedback had been discarded in favor of software the general manager had used during previous employment with a major corporate.

12 months down the track the business was slowly retrieving the situation, tracking invoices, and monitoring performance weekly.

Having targeted 200 hours per week into product at an average gross profit of $100 per hour, the key to achieving the desired profit lies in comparing invoices with the TARI® benchmark – preferably at the time of quoting – as well as comparing actual with target weekly – on the grounds that it is possible to catch up on a bad week but much more difficult to catch up on a bad month.

### Performance Summary Ending Week 6

| Day | Sales $ A | Cost of Materials B | Gross Profit C = A - B | Gross Profit % D = C / A | No. Of Hours E | Ave GP per Hour F = C / E |
|---|---|---|---|---|---|---|
| 1 | 6,000 | 3,200 | 2,800 | 47 | 40 | 70 |
| 5 | 28,800 | 14,800 | 14,000 | 49 | 135 | 104 |
| Total | 34,800 | 18,000 | 16,800 | 48 | 175 | 96 |
| Total b/f | 220,000 | 108,000 | 112,000 | 51 | 1,098 | 102 |
| Total c/f | 254,800 | 126,000 | 128,800 | 50.5 | 1,273 | 101 |
| Target | 240,000 | 120,000 | 120,000 | 50 | 1,200 | 100 |
| Variance | +14,800 | +6,000 | +8,800 | +0.5 | +73 | +1 |

Over time that I came to see a business could be likened to a wheel with the hub turning according to the level of output activity (productivity) and the spokes representing the various departments or functions such as personnel, production, marketing administration, finance, IT systems and so forth.

For a wheel to operate in a balanced way with a minimum of friction, the spokes need to be of equal length. Should one or more of the spokes protrude ahead of the others, the impact is transmitted to the hub.

If the wheel is targeted to move at an agreed speed (output) matching available resources, the extent of any change in speed (output) is reflected at the hub by comparison with TARI® on an invoice-by-invoice basis and by comparison with the overall weekly and accumulative target.

It is the sustained focus on movement at the hub (output and gross profit contribution per unit of output) that tends to become self-fulfilling, not only for manufacturing or service oriented sectors, but for wholesale and retail business as well, as the following real-life case study illustrates.

# CASE STUDY 6:

# WHOLESALER NETS $2.5M IN 10+ MONTHS

A management buy-out of a company being sold for lack of profitable performance, illustrates what can happen when targets are broken into digestible proportions.

Having assisted with a management buyout of a wholesaling company supplying ships at ports around the coastline, I agreed to take on the role of Chairman until the company settled into its stride.

Once the buyout was finalized, I called a meeting of senior executives to work out a strategy for the year ahead. Sales were around $50 million with gross profit running at a low 20% and net profit a dubious 1%.

"What is the average sale?" I asked, looking around the boardroom table. There was silence and a shuffling of feet.

"There's no such thing in this business," smiled the General Manager, somewhat indulgently.

"Why do you say that?" I asked.

"Well, a major customer like one of the Queens might order $150,000 worth or we'll get a tug boat ordering bread and milk for $50. No way can there be an average sale in this business."

"There's one thing for sure" I replied, "if you don't know the average sale you certainly won't improve it." I recounted an example of a typical hardware store with some 7,000 product lines, ranging from $1,000 chainsaws to 50-cent packets of screws. The gross profit per average sale was $20 and once it had been identified, the daily average achieved would be noted in large characters on the whiteboard in the employee's staff room. It provided a daily update and helped sustain focus on where the rubber meets the road.

"As we don't even have a record of the number of sales made, we need to start tracking the sales and gross profit for every vessel supplied. In time, that will build up a more accurate picture."

I pressed for a target of 25% gross profit margin with recording to commence immediately.

As the weeks passed, information was processed and sent back to each branch in a format that could be pinned up on the lunchroom notice board. The results of each representative were shown, highlighting the number of sales made and the average gross profit achieved for the preceding week and accumulatively for the weeks to date.

A sample analysis of past sales quickly established the average sale had been in the region of $5,000, following which, the focus shifted from vague generalizations about how to improve an existing 20% gross profit of $50m sales, to how to achieve a gross profit of 25% of a $5,000 sale. In reality the $5,000 was a statistical average and actual sales ranged widely. By refocusing to a manageable average sale of $5,000, it made it possible for management and representatives to target the real objective, which was to improve gross profit from the equivalent of $1,000 to $1,250 per average sale.

It was a question that became the focus of subsequent management meetings resulting in simple and achievable objectives that could be carried out in each branch.

Within two months, reports filtered back from branches revealing different methods adopted to improve the gross profit per sale.

One northern branch handling coal vessels took brochures from the local jeweler on board the ships and sold opals to the crew, increasing the average gross profit by $300 a sale.

Another branch made a deal with the local video outlet and sold videos to the crew, increasing the average gross profit by $200 per sale.

With the increased gross profit flowing directly to the bottom line and gross profit margins continuing to climb with the support of improved buying and focusing on items that attracted higher margins, net profit rose steeply, in turn strengthening the cash flow.

Quarterly management workshops imparted additional input, training branch management in planning, targeting, and monitoring performance, providing a means of sharing marketing skills, developing more effective and timely collection of the proceeds, and sharpening techniques of purchasing to reduce costs and control inventory.

From the time of the management buyout to the end of the financial year – a period covering ten and half months, the average gross profit per sale increased by $250, which on 10,000 sales, resulted in a net profit of $2.5m.

The success attracted the attention of stockbrokers and within eighteen months from the time of buyout, the company was listed on the stock exchange providing a handsome paper gain for the vending shareholders as well as additional cash for funding expansion.

It was at this point that I stepped down from the Chairman's role, handing over to one of the three newly appointed non-executive directors.

Given the need to report to the stock exchange and deal with the more burdensome regulatory matters of a listed company, the

# TARI ® The Key to Hidden Profit

Board in its wisdom replaced the existing chief accountant with a more sophisticated company secretary from a major accounting firm.

Unfamiliar with the software that had been introduced to handle the week-by-week reports to and from the branches, he dispensed with them and reverted to the traditional monthly reporting syndrome contained in a 120-page Board Pack that arrived three weeks after the month to which the contents referred.

The branches continued to send in their weekly reports but Head Office merely filed them without providing any feedback of results for posting on the branch notice board. Within six months, gross profits fell from a high of 28% to a terminal 20%.

Lack of focus on where the rubber meets the road, brought the company close to its knees, and within a year of listing I was asked to return as Chairman.

---

Chasing an annual target of say $50m, can only be achieved by small steps, with each day taking care of itself. Thus the focus on gross profit sale by sale and the focus on the number of sales week by week.

The average sale of $5,000 was purely a statistic. It is unlikely there was such a sale, but it was eminently more digestible than focusing on $50 million.

$5,000 could be comprehended and focused by the branch managers, although each branch had a different average sale depending on the size of vessel loading at the port.

The simple objectives called for each branch to target a number of sales together with an average gross profit per sale, which converted to their TARI®. It then became a matter of working with the reps to develop ways and means of achieving increased added value per sale.

Breaking down the total into its constituent parts that could be readily grasped and developing a target along with ways and means of achieving it, drew on the combined input of branch personnel, who responded accordingly to achieve outstanding results.

# Wholesaler Nets $2.5m in 10+ Months

It was revealing to hear from the branch managers at the quarterly workshops the different methods used by reps to boost the added value per sale, knowing their results would be published on the notice board and promulgated in the company newsletter.

An interesting aspect of this case was the extensive monthly reporting system that had been established under the previous owners – a multinational group with several hundred subsidiaries, each providing a monthly Board Pack covering traditional financial statements, aging of accounts receivables, details of staffing, pertinent comments from each branch and so forth, But nothing about number of sales made, average sale or gross profit per sale, overall or by branch or representative.

Following my return as chairman, the system of weekly feedback of number of sales and average gross profit per sale was reinstalled, much to the initial skepticism of certain board members. However, the time came, when one of their first questions at the commencement of board meetings was "how are we going with TARI®?"

The following real-life case study of a small retailer illustrates what can happen when focus is sustained day by day on the two key drivers of activity (number of sales) and $rate (gross profit per sale).

# CASE STUDY 7:

# JEWELER'S CHANGED FOCUS TURNS RED INTO BLACK

**D**ependant on passing tourist trade, this Jeweler found it impossible to do more than cover costs, let alone make a profit.

Volume was up last year but the bottom line showed a loss. Discounting had been too high. Given their position on a twenty-minute tourist stopover, it was perhaps understandable the focus tended to be a sale at any price. Nevertheless, it was thought that next year things would be better because of a potential pick-up in tourism.

I was assisting their very able external accountant with client interviews at the time.

"How can you help us?" the jeweler asked the accountant. "You're an accountant not a jeweler."

"I can't help you with the jewelry side of the business" the accountant replied, "but I can help you with the management side if you care to cooperate in what is known as the TARI® process."

"What's that?" husband and wife chorused.

"It's essentially a matter of focusing on two key performance indicators that have been found to make all the difference between success and mediocre performance in business."

"Tell us more," said the husband

"Well, as a first step perhaps you can tell me your average sale?" the accountant asked.

"Average sale...what do you reckon? " he asked his wife who shook her head.

"Probably about $30, maybe more or less." he guessed.

"What about the average gross profit per sale?"

"Well I suppose if the average sale is $30 and the mark-up is 100%, the average gross profit would be $15. But why ask?"

"Because the $15 gross profit covers your expenses and profit. The other $15 covers the cost of purchases and as you are in business for yourself and not your suppliers, it is what is left over after you have paid them that matters.

"But I don't get the drift. What's the point of knowing the average gross profit?"

"Because it's difficult to improve on an amount that you don't know"

"Hmmm"

"Well we could find out by looking at the cash register sales for a selection of say, 6 days that you believe to be representative of sales," the accountant suggested and with some reluctance, the jeweler agreed to fax sample information the following week.

By the time they met again, the accountant had prepared the following analysis.

## Analysis of a Representative Sample of Sales on 6 days during past period [4]

| Day | Sale Price A | Cost of Goods Sold B | Gross Profit C = (A − B) | Gross Profit % D = C/A | No of Sales E | Ave GP per Sale F = C/E |
|---|---|---|---|---|---|---|
| 26/01 | 1,100 | 715 | 385 | 35 | 32 | 12.00 |
| 13/02 | 1,400 | 868 | 532 | 38 | 59 | 9.00 |
| 10/04 | 1,250 | 725 | 525 | 42 | 46 | 11.50 |
| 15/12 | 1,500 | 900 | 600 | 40 | 55 | 11.00 |
| 17/08 | 1,360 | 898 | 462 | 34 | 32 | 14.50 |
| 21/09 | 1,290 | 800 | 490 | 38 | 49 | 10.00 |
| Total | 7,900 | 4,906 | 2,994 | 38 | 273 | 11.00 |

Surprised to see the range in gross profit per sale the jeweler asked, "Where do we go from here?"

"Well let's start tracking from tomorrow by comparing the average gross profit with a target average gross profit per sale which we call TARI®, short for target average rate index. It is a benchmark.

"All you need to do is note the sales and cost of goods sold and the number of sales made on this sheet and fax it in once a week. We'll put it into the computer and email it back the next day giving you an up-to-date fix on where you are at compared with target."

The accountant handed him several pre-printed sheets.

---

[4] It is worth noting that the sample analysis could have extracted the number of items sold per sale, seeing that a sale frequently includes more than one item. In the case of comparing two or more retail outlets of similar products, the items per sale can be a very useful comparison of merchandising techniques. Volume of sales can be similar, but gross profit per sale noticeably different, because one outlet is more into added value per sale than the other.

TARI ® The Key to Hidden Profit

"What's my target then?" the jeweler asked.

"Good question" replied the accountant. "We need to decide that before you go."

After projecting the likely expenses and adding a desirable net profit for the year ahead, they divided the resulting target gross profit by the estimated number of sales to arrive at a TARI®.

## Planning and Targeting Ahead

| | | |
|---|---|---|
| A | Target Total Expenses | $125,000 |
| B | Target Net Profit | $75,000 |
| C = A + B | Target Gross Profit | $200,000 |
| D | Target No. Sales | 15,000 |
| E = C / D | TARI® = 200,000 / 15,000 | $13.33 |
| F | Target Gross Profit Margin % | 40% |
| G = C / F | Target Sales = 200,000 / 40% | $500,000 |
| H = G – C | Target Cost of Goods Sold | $300,000 |

"Once we get some feedback we can adjust targets as required to achieve the desired bottom line." The accountant reached for the Action Sheet and began to spell out who was to what by when.

Several months went by before I received the following report from the accountant.

*Re Jeweler:*

"He likes the idea of monitoring progress weekly and is currently running ahead of target. The reasons he gives are as follows:

*'Likes the idea of having a yardstick by which to gauge performance on weekly basis
It gives his management function some structure
Information obtained has assisted in:*

1. *Developing product mix (to improve gross profit)*
2. *Formulating a pricing policy*
3. *Obtaining feedback on the effectiveness of marketing activity*
4. *Obtaining feedback on effectiveness of sales staff*
5. *Obtaining a better understanding of the cycles that affect his business'*

*He believes 'the process has been valuable and helped increase profit and give direction.'"*

I subsequently learned the jeweler had stood up at a client taxation seminar held by the accountant and spoken enthusiastically of the help he had received.

"It was a bit embarrassing really," the accountant explained, but as the conversation took place by phone, I was unable to see if he was blushing.

---

The accountant did not push for access to historical data to analyze past performance. He knew from experience the data would be fragmented, tax oriented and unreliable as a guide to targeting future performance. So what was the point? Best to start with a sample of sales that would provide some background data as a basis for planning ahead, and move on to capture actual data going forward so the real picture would emerge over the coming weeks.

The sample does not pinpoint productivity of staff in the same way as non-retail business where the key activity relates more to man or machine hours. Where data is available, it is possible to make comparisons with other like retail businesses to assess staff effectiveness. Known as Interfirm Comparison, the data will normally provide an indication of sales per person employed.

Many retailers maintain records of number of sales made and can easily derive their average sale. However, there are numerous occasions on which discounts are applied in an attempt to increase the number of sales and boost the overall gross profit. Caught up in day-to-day merchandising, buying and restocking, supervising staff, serving customers, banking receipts and paying bills, it is not difficult to lose track of the gross profit per sale and in doing so, lose sight of the bottom line.

A day-by-day comparison of gross profit per sale with TARI® together with a comparison of weekly and accumulative total of number of sales against target, kept the jeweler focused and motivated.

## Performance Summary ending Week 10

| Day | Sales $ A | Cost of Purchases B | Gross Profit C = A - B | Gross Profit % D = C / A | No. Of Sales E | Ave GP per Sale F = C / E |
|---|---|---|---|---|---|---|
| 1 | 2,000 | 1,200 | 800 | 40 | 65 | 12.31 |
| 2 | 1,750 | 1,000 | 750 | 43 | 50 | 15.00 |
| 3 | 1,155 | 700 | 435 | 48 | 33 | 13.00 |
| 4 | 1,085 | 650 | 435 | 40 | 35 | 12,43 |
| 5 | 1,800 | 1,050 | 750 | 42 | 45 | 16.67 |
| Total | 7,790 | 4,600 | 3,190 | 41 | 228 | 13.99 |
| Total b/f | 47,000 | 27,000 | 20,000 | 42.5 | 1,425 | 14.04 |
| Total c/f | 54,790 | 31,600 | 23,190 | 42.3 | 1,653 | 14.03 |
| Target | 50,000 | 30,000 | 20,000 | 40 | 1,500 | 13.33 |
| Variance | +4,790 | +1,600 | +3,190 | +2.3 | +153 | +0.70 |

This brings us to a real-life case study of a very small business that drives home the importance of maintaining focus where the rubber meets the road.

# CASE STUDY 8:

# UPMARKET CAFÉ LEARNS HOW TO STAY ON TRACK

**T**wo friends in the hospitality industry open a café in an upmarket suburb and strike problems on the opening day. Fortunately, they had a wise mentor.

The day arrived for opening. Jane and Ruth had combined forces to prepare for this day when their new cafe would open its doors. Everything was brand-new, from the cafe building itself to the tables, chairs, cutlery, crockery, and sparkling kitchen, replete with the latest equipment and shining extraction flue over a gleaming white cooking range and oven.

They had prepared the menu very carefully. Their cafe was to be smart and casual as fitted the suburb, and the menu had to fit the image, gourmet but not exclusively so, with prices pitched to match the type of customer they hoped to attract.

In addition to their combined experience as executive chef and assistant manager of a major city hotel, they were particularly fortunate to have a CPA friend who had insisted they prepare a focus-based financial projection of their expectations. Their projections were as follows:

## Planning & Targeting Future Performance

| | | |
|---|---|---|
| A | Total Expenses: Rent + part-time wages + leasing of fittings + insurance + telephone etc | $125,000 |
| B | Target Net Profit | $85,000 |
| C = A + B | Target Gross Profit (70% of sales) | $210,000 |
| D = C / 70% | Target Sales $210,000 / 70% | $300,000 |
| E | Estimated Ave Sale per customer (or 'cover') | $10 |
| F = E x 70% | Target Ave Gross Profit per cover = TARI® | $7 |
| G = C / F | Target no Customers $210,000 / $7 | 30,000 |
| H | Days open | 338 |
| I = G / H | Ave no of customers per day | 89 |
| J = I x F | Target Average gross profit per day (89 x $7) | $623 |
| K = I x F x H | Check annual gross profit target (89 x $7 x 338) | $210,574 |

## Upmarket Café Learns How to Stay on Track

The opening day brought a touch of mayhem. Over 150 customers were served, one part-timer failed to turn up, the health inspector condemned the flue over the stove, and the dishwasher overflowed across the kitchen floor.

As if that was not enough, when they checked the takings against the number of customers (referred to as 'covers' in the trade), they discovered the average gross profit worked out at $6.13.

Concluding that this was mainly due to the sale of menu items at the lower end of the scale and determined to get closer to their TARI® of $7, they sat down at midnight and rewrote the menu.

Failing to reach target the next day, they again stayed up late and rewrote the menu and again the third and the fourth day until they got it right.

Eighteen months later, enjoying a coffee in the café, I asked Ruth how things were working out. She told me they now employed six part-timers and she had the cost of provisions down from 30% to 23% of sales by buying directly from the market. They were still monitoring the average gross profit and the number of sales, daily and accumulatively as well as keeping a firm grip on expenses.

---

Serving the best snacks and brewing the best coffee in town would have attracted any number of customers to their café, but at a price. In the case of this café, the difference from the norm was that the proprietors knew the financial outcome they wanted, and what was needed to attain it.

Targeting a net profit of $85,000 on top of all expenses to achieve an annual gross profit of $210,000 and breaking it down across an estimated number of customers into a target gross profit per serve (cover) is the easy part of the exercise.

The real difficulty is the follow through. Not many show the determination of these two proprietors prepared to sit down after a tiring day and make it happen.

It becomes obvious that sustaining the connection between the invoice and bottom line calls for a disciplined and ongoing commitment. Occasions will arise when the value and the point of the exercise will be questioned. It is then we need to be reminded of the underlying principle at work.

What exactly was the principle at work? It was a question that plagued me in my early days of working with numerous businesses across the country. To know it worked was one thing, but why?

The following real-life case study helped me resolve the 'why?'

# CASE STUDY 9:

# DIESEL REPAIR SHOP RESCUED FROM SAND-UP HILL COUNTRY

**A** top sales engineer deciding on a change of lifestyle takes over a diesel repair business. As the business heads into liquidation, his wife discovers the way out.

After two days conducting workshops for 40 business clients of an accounting practice, I was ready to fly home, when John, one of the partners said, "there's one client I really wanted to come to attend the workshop. He needs it more than any of the others, but he refused on the grounds he was too flat-out. Fact is, he is heading down the tubes faster than a rabbit down a burrow and needs help badly. When his wife rang to apologize, I told her if she could get him into the office at 7 a.m., I would try to persuade you to stay another night."

He went on to tell me the client and his wife had sold their city home two years prior to buying a diesel repair business with a 3 bedroom home and a few acres of land attached, mortgaging themselves heavily in the process. The husband had been a sales engineer with a major company in the city, but loved to get his hands dirty playing with diesel engines. Unless a miracle occurred, they looked like being bankrupted within a matter of weeks.

Although trying to sleep in a motel room fronting a noisy highway was no inducement, I agreed to stay the extra night.

In the morning, I headed for the conference room at John's office and found the couple already seated at the table, the wife making small talk with John. It was obvious from the outset the husband was not interested in advice from a so-called expert and resented being there. In his mind, he was well aware the solution to their financial problems lay back in the workshop fixing up diesel engines of trucks and fishing boats. That is where the action was and that is where the money was to be made if they were to have any chance at all at clawing back their debt-ridden business.

As he sat hunched over the table, head in hands, she smiled an apology for his attitude.

"How busy are you?" I asked.

"Very busy" she replied

"What do you charge for an hour's work?"

"$30" she said.

"How many hours do you work in the average week?"

"Oh I don't know exactly" she replied, "but he works very long hours."

"Well let's say 60 hours a week, or 3,000 hours a year," I ventured

"He works day and night and all weekends" she said nudging him to respond. He emitted a faint groan.

I wrote on a sheet of paper in front of them:
3,000 hours x $30 = $90,000

"Did you get anything like this from hours charged last year?"

"Oh no!" she exclaimed, "Nothing like that"

"Ignoring the parts, they actually billed $30,000" John said, reading from the tax papers.

## Diesel Repair Shop Rescued from Sand-Up Hill Country

"We certainly didn't!" she said adamantly.

"Well you did bill $30,000. You received $15,000 cash and the balance of $15,000 is in accounts receivable," said John.

"Accounts receivable? Do you mean farmers?" she queried referring to the great majority of their customers.

"If you billed $30,000, and worked 3,000 hours you must have charged closer to $10 an hour," I said

"No, I do all the billing, and we never charge less than $30 an hour" she replied.

"In that case, you charged out only 1000 hours to bill $30,000 - or roughly 20 hours a week. You must have many interruptions?" I quietly suggested.

"Oh yes, the phone never stops" she said

"Don't you take messages?"

"Yes, but they're all urgent and they want to talk to him right away"

I wrote PHONE on a sheet. "Any other interruptions?"

"Oh yes, the farmers" she said.

"What about the farmers?" I asked

"Well they walk straight into the workshop and start talking. Maybe they want an exhaust pipe welded or something. He has to stop what he is doing and attend to them and afterwards they say 'how much' and he says 'a couple of dollars' and they say 'put it on the account'. And farmers do talk slowly" she added.

I wrote FARMERS on the sheet. "Anything else?"

"Well, there's the garage mechanics" she said

"What about them?"

"They come straight into the workshop and ask for advice."

"Why do they do that?"

"Well he's a top diesel man, the best in the region. He can pick a problem in an engine as the truck comes up the hill to the workshop, just by listening to it." She looked at her husband with a tinge of pride. Hunched over the table, he was silently shaking his head, anxious to be back in sand-up-hill country.

"Do you mean he can do the work in half the time of the average mechanic?" I asked.

"A quarter" she said.

"In that case he could charge $60 an hour and still be cheaper than the average mechanic."

"Bullshit" rang through the air like a shotgun, expressing pent up disgust and disagreement over what was taking place, as though to suggest that if he charged $60 an hour he would be laughed out of business overnight.

Seeking a solution to what seemed to be a hopeless situation, I addressed the wife.

"Do you think that if the interruptions could be fixed, such as putting netting around the workshop to force farmers and garage mechanics through the office entrance, and educating customers concerning his availability to answer phone calls only at certain times, that you could extract 7 chargeable hours a day?

"If you could do that for a 5-day week plus say 5 hours on Saturday, it would give 40 chargeable hours. And if you upped the $30 to $40, that would bring in $1,600 a week or close to $86,000 a year from hours charged?"

"If something could be done about the interruptions, I suppose we could." she nodded somewhat uncertainly.

We used an Action Sheet to spell out who was to do what. She agreed to accept responsibility for the 40 hours by $40 a week and John the accountant elected to assist in getting the accounts receivables collected and arranging for netting to be placed around the workshop.

Saying goodbye to John later, I expressed a sense of my inadequacy concerning the interview. She in particular, I felt, was expecting something really out of the hat from the visiting 'expert'.

A few months later, I bumped into John at a conference. "How are they going?" I asked.

"Keeping their noses in front. The simple formula seems to be working", said John with a smile.

About eighteen months later, John told me they were out of their troubles and going well. "By the way" he asked, "what did you mean when you told me he was in sand-up-hill country?"

"That's the place where you shovel all day with a shovel full of holes. It's not very productive, but you do go home feeling something good must have happened because you are exhausted from a hard day's work"

"Oh I see." said John. "Sounds like a typical tax practice to me."

> Because this particular interview took place very early in my research, some time passed before I came to understand and grasp the importance of what had transpired. In reviewing the interview, I recalled the target set for her was a weekly one. That was a little unusual bearing in mind that at the time, I had never previously thought in terms of less than monthly feedback. Nevertheless, I could imagine her informing the husband on the last day of the month, probably around midnight as he eased his tired body between the sheets, that he had only completed a 140 hours this month and would need to do 180 next month to catch up.
>
> Apart from the unlikelihood of catching up on a 20-hour backlog, I could only guess his response to such an approach. However, there was a good chance of catching up on a weeks' deficit of say 4 hours. Weekly feedback was obviously important and that would have played a part in their recovery, although that in itself was not an adequate explanation for the turnaround.
>
> There was something more, and it only occurred to me much later. In addition to ordering parts, preparing invoices, chasing debtors, handling demands of the bank and suppliers, coping with phone calls and all the other multitude of events in the day-to-day life of business, she was also chief cook and bottle washer, bed maker and mother to two small children. She was doing everything she could as best as she could, and all the time fighting a growing sense of depression as she saw their life savings fading away with no light at the end of the tunnel.
>
> The truth was that although every activity mattered in one way or another, she - along with 95% of businesses - had no focus on what really mattered in the business. It was only when she focused on extracting 40 billable hours a week from her husband and invoicing them out at $40 an hour plus the cost of parts that the business began to get back on track.

Simple enough, yet so vitally important.

By this time I was aware that comparison of actual with potential performance was the simplest approach to pinpointing levels of productivity. It invariably captured the client's interest enough to look further for explanations.

However, having been nurtured on traditional financial statements the importance of weekly feedback did not really take root so easily. I had thought my push for more frequent feedback of quarterly and even monthly statements, comparing actual with budget, was a fairly advanced concept at the time.

The methodology used in this case to pinpoint actual versus potential output, gave way to using invoice analysis as a more effective means of identifying productivity.

More on that in the case studies that follow.

CASE STUDY 10:

# GARMENT MAKER MULTIPLIES NET PROFIT BY 700%

**C**aught up in the traditional approach to pricing, the CEO and Sales Manager are excited when they see the possibilities open up with the application of TARI®

A partner of the accounting practice drove me to his client's factory and introduced me to a smilingly alert proprietor and his attractive designer wife. After the formalities, we settled down to look at their method of pricing garments.

"We go to the larger retail outlets and check the selling price of say, a pair of shorts, then we'll come back and work out how much we can make them for in addition to making a profit for us as well as the retailer."

TARI ® The Key to Hidden Profit

The proprietor tabled several costing sheets listing the various garments made along with the estimated minutes to make, the material type, size and cost along with accessories, such as buttons, zips, cotton thread, buckles and so forth. A percentage was added to the cost of material and accessories and a rate per minute applied to the time. The result was known as the Cost to which a 40% mark-up was then applied.

"Why 40%?" I asked.

"That's to cover the overheads and profit." he replied

"How many are employed in making the garments?"

"We employ 30 full-time as well as subcontractors."

"What level of productivity are you getting from the staff?"

"Ninety three percent" he said proudly. "We have the completed garments tallied each day and know exactly how many minutes have been put into them."

93% was surprising. "You're sure the estimated times for garments are not too generous?"

"No, we test the times across several mock-ups to work out the best way of handling the flow of work beforehand."

"Let's see what the average gross profit contribution per minute was last year." I went to the whiteboard.

### Exhibit A: Establishing Gross Profit per Minute for past year

| Item | $ | Minutes to Make | Cents per Minute | Comment |
|---|---|---|---|---|
| **Sales** | 6,000,000 | 9,000,000 | 66.7 | Internal staff = 3,000,000 minutes Subcontractors = 6,000,000 mins |
| Cost of Materials + Subcontractors at 20c a minute (6m x 20c) | 2,100,000 + 1,200,000 | | | Materials only + Subcontractors only |

Garment Maker Multiplies Net Profit by 700%

| | | | | |
|---|---|---|---|---|
| Total of Materials + Contractors | 3,300,00 | 9,000,000 | 36.7 | $3,300,000/ 9,000,000 mins |
| **Gross Profit** | 2,700,000 | 9,000,000 | 30.0 | $2,700,000/ 9,000,000 mins |
| Expenses (includes wages of in-house 3,000,000 mins) | 2,600,000 | | 28.9 | $2,600,000/ 9,000,000 mins |
| **Net Profit** | 100,000 | | 1.1 | $100,000/ 9,000,000 mins |

"Let's see how that compares with a sample of the current range of garments," I suggested, drawing up columns on the whiteboard, as he made ready to call out the numbers.

**Exhibit B: Comparison of Average Gross Profit cents per minute with Sample of Garments**

| Garment Style No. | Inv. Price $ A | Mat'l Cost $ B | Gross Profit $ C = A − B | GP % D = C / A | No. Minutes E | Ave GP Cents per Minute F = C / E |
|---|---|---|---|---|---|---|
| 114 | 12 | 5 | 7 | 58 | 25 | 28 |
| 119 | 14 | 6 | 8 | 57 | 27 | 30 |
| 126 | 19 | 8 | 11 | 58 | 27 | 41 |
| 132 | 18 | 6 | 12 | 67 | 20 | 60 |
| 144 | 16 | 9 | 7 | 44 | 27 | 26 |
| 153 | 15 | 7 | 8 | 53 | 32 | 25 |

| 167 | 30 | 12 | 18 | 60 | 26 | 70 |
|-----|----|----|----|----|----|----|
| 175 | 33 | 14 | 19 | 58 | 34 | 56 |

The owner pointed to the 30 cents average gross profit in Exhibit A. "How come we have an overall average gross profit of 30 cents a minute compared with a range of up to 70 cents in the sample?"

"Doesn't the 30 cents depend on the number of units sold in each style, so that if more are sold of say, styles 144 and 153, the average will fall away?" replied the in-house accountant.

We agreed it may be informative to multiply out the number sold in each style by the minutes and calculate the total gross profit per garment, but it would be a lengthy process. We moved on to consider the significance of the variety of gross profit contributions per minute stemming from the different garments.

The sales manager who had been called in to observe the exercise was especially intrigued. "Does that mean that if I sell 1,000 units of 167, we get a gross profit contribution of $18,000 and if I sell the same number of 114 we get a gross profit of $7,000, even though both have taken up much the same time to make?"

I assured him that was the case.

"If I'd known that last week, I could have won an order for 1,000 of 167. As it is, we lost it because we could not get the price down enough to beat the competition. Our policy only allowed me to drop 10%, and I needed to drop 20%. Even with 20%, we would still have made a gross profit contribution of $14,400. Boss this is great stuff!" he exclaimed, "It's going to make all the difference to our sales. I shall now know what to push and what not to push."

I pointed out that as long as7 he kept the overall gross profit target in view, to which all styles contributed, then all would be well. The key for an increased bottom line was to push the styles with the higher contribution and work out ways and means of raising the gross profit per minute from the lower contributors by better buying of materials or more efficient processes.

# Garment Maker Multiplies Net Profit by 700%

With that, we agreed to project an increased net profit for the year ahead, upping the target average gross contribution rate per minute from 30 cents to 35 cents. I explained that we would refer to the 35 cents as the target average rate index - TARI® - a benchmark against which the contribution per minute from the various styles would be compared quote by quote or invoice by invoice.

Starting with the expenses, we ran through all the items from the previous year, maintaining staff numbers at the same level with an appropriate increase in wages. Maintaining in-house productivity at 93% and increasing the subcontractor minutes by 1 million from 6 million to 7 million minutes, to meet anticipated increase in sales, we summarized on the whiteboard as follows:

### Exhibit C: Planning and Targeting Performance

| | | |
|---|---|---|
| A | Expenses (excluding subcontractors) | $2,800,000 |
| B | Net Profit | $700,000 |
| C = A + B | Gross Profit | $3,500,000 |
| D | Target Ave Rate Index (TARI®) | 35 cents |
| E = C / D | Estimated number of minutes required ($3,500,000 / 35 cents) | 10,000,000 mins |
| F | In-house minutes at 93% productivity | 3,000,000 mins |
| G = E - F | Mins required from subcontractors | 7,000,000 mins |

"That's a big increase in net profit on last year don't you think?" asked the proprietor

"I reckon we can get it" the sales manager smiled enthusiastically, "Now that I know where we are going, we can soon work out what we need to sell to get there."

I explained the key to success was to capture invoiced sales, gross profit, and minutes weekly and accumulatively for comparison with target.

During the ensuing three years, the firm went on to treble sales to $18 million, boosting net profit to $1 million, and using the funds to build a state of the art factory containing the very latest technology coupled with outstanding working conditions for the employees. It was then that import duty was reduced to the point where cheaply produced garments from overseas created such pressure that had the proprietors lacked a clear idea of where to direct their energies, they would have gone under. As it was, in order to sustain profitable growth, they subcontracted offshore.

---

Six new and important aspects of this business were highlighted in this case:

1. Identifying the average gross profit per minute ;
2. The range of gross profits per minute in different styles;
3. The potential of that information for the Sales Manager;
4. The inadequacy of an inflexible discount policy;
5. Targeting an increase of 5 cents per minute from 30 to 35 was achievable;
6. The clarity achieved by of separating the cost of materials and outsourced work from the targeted gross profit necessary to cover internal operating costs + profit.

The gross profit per minute per style of garment (Exhibit A) coming as new information to management was not surprising, given the standard approach to costing and pricing, which includes a rate per minute of time plus a percentage mark-up on materials and accessories prior to a further 40% mark-up to cover overheads and profit.

# Garment Maker Multiplies Net Profit by 700%

> Inclusion of mark-up on materials coupled with additional markups – usually based on the previous year's performance - masks the contribution per unit of activity, in this case a minute of time, and in doing so, obscures an important decision-making tool.
>
> The following real-life case study shows how gross profit contribution per key unit of activity is obtained from invoice analysis and how that information can be used to pinpoint the actual level of activity (productivity) in a business.

## CASE STUDY 11:

# SWITCHBOARD MANUFACTURER CLIMBS INTO THE BLACK

**W**hile senior management held to conflicting views about the cause of declining profitability, a representative sample of invoices helped pinpoint the problem in a matter of minutes.

When the financial statements finally emerged, four months after the end of the financial year, they only confirmed what was already known: the business was losing ground and fast.

The cause of the decline was hard to pin point. Everybody in the place, ranging from the CEO to the tea girl seemed to have a different point of view.

The production manager put the problem down to the new computer system that had been installed at great expense eighteen months earlier and was still being worked on by the consultant that sold the deal as being the latest and the best on the market. The software pumped out information by the ream, but no one could interpret it.

The marketing manager felt the problem lay in production, where time sheets were no longer kept since the new computer system was installed and there was no control over the times anymore. As a result, quotes had become more and more uncompetitive.

The accountant was of the opinion the new system was really quite effective and that it could give any variety of reports, but that the consultant was yet to complete certain adjustments. As a result, he was unable to extract agency lines that were purchased for resale and formed about one third of total sales from the manufactured parts. Concerning the loss, he agreed that was serious, but was outside his area of responsibility. He considered the problem was most likely to be the economic environment not being conducive to the current product range.

The CEO said the business was in need of new plant and equipment if it was to remain competitive, but that called for capital injection, and given the state of the accounts, the bank had severely restricted all credit facilities.

Reviewing the reports currently provided I noted they summarized results in traditional management accounting format complete with under and over recoveries from labor and materials, direct and indirect allocations of expenses and so forth. Even with interpretation, the reports lacked relevance to the pressing needs of management for a wood's view.

Gross profit of $5,000,000 – recalculated as sales less cost of materials - failed to cover expenses, resulting in a net loss of $200,000.

Analysis of a representative sample of invoices recast as Sales – Materials, revealed an average gross profit per production hour of $155.

## Exhibit A: Recasts the same jobs with Gross Profit calculated as Sales – Materials

| Job No | Sales A | Materials D | Gross Profit G = A – D | Gross Profit % G / A | Hours H | Ave GP per Hour G / H |
|---|---|---|---|---|---|---|
| 345 | 3,600 | 1,750 | 1,850 | 51 | 4.84 | 382 |
| 348 | 2,200 | 660 | 1,540 | 70 | 12 | 128 |
| 351 | 2,000 | 1,536 | 464 | 23 | 7 | 66 |
| 356 | 960 | 90 | 870 | 91 | 5.8 | 150 |
| 360 | 1,900 | 310 | 1,590 | 84 | 13 | 122 |
| 362 | 2,050 | 396 | 1,654 | 34 | 8.8 | 188 |
| Total | 12,710 | 4,742 | 7,968 | 63 | 51.4 | 155 |

Dividing the total gross profit of $5,000,000 by the average gross profit of $155 per hour in the sample provided a close guesstimate of hours charged out for the period.

$5,000,000/$155 = 32,258 hrs

Paid Hours = 65,000 hrs

Productivity = 32,258/65,000 = 50%

**Or 4 hours output for every 8 hrs paid.**

The CEO looked shocked, the marketing manager nodded agreement, the production manager frowned in disbelief, and the accountant queried the reliability of the invoice sample.

TARI ® The Key to Hidden Profit

I pointed out that regardless of the reliability of the sample, there was little to be gained by spending time and money delving into historical records, the true situation would be revealed over the next few weeks as we tracked actual against plan.

It was time to plan ahead by projecting expenses, adding the desired net profit and targeting an increase in productive hours from 4 hours to 5 hours per 8-hour day or 62.5%.

### Exhibit B: Planning and Targeting

|   | Item | Plan |
|---|------|------|
| A | Expenses (excluding materials) | $5,200,0000 |
| B | Target net profit | $300,000 |
| C = A + B | Target gross profit | $5,500,000 |
| D | Paid production hours | 65,000 hours |
| E = D x 62.5% | Target chargeable hours based on achieving 5 hrs per 8 hour day or 62.5% of paid hours | 40,625 hours |
| F = C / E | TARI® | $135 |
| G = C / 45 | Average weekly gross profit target | $122,222 |
| H = E / 45 | Average weekly hours | 905 hrs |

Because of the targeted increase in chargeable hours, the TARI® of $135 was $20 under the average gross profit per hour of $155 from the invoice sample. This led to heated debate about which benchmark should be adopted.

I pointed out that it would be unwise to track against a benchmark lower than the one showing up in the sample. To put their

## Switchboard Manufacturer Climbs into the Black

minds at ease, we analyzed an additional sample of 20 invoices and came up with $155. Using $155 meant an additional $800,000 if they could improve productivity from 4 hrs to 5 hrs a day. They would be on track to achieve a gross profit of $6,300,000.

"I don't see how we are going to get the work?" said the CEO to a chorus of agreement.

"Why don't we just start and see what happens" I suggested, knowing from experience that once they started tracking quotes against the TARI® benchmark of $155 and the weekly target of 905 hours, they would achieve the competitive advantage necessary to secure additional work.

Tracking invoiced sales, gross profit, and hourly rates weekly and accumulatively, slowly but surely brought the business back on track.

Quotations by Marketing were compared with the TARI® benchmark for the rate per hour before they were sent out and again before they were committed to production. Rates that showed less than $155 were examined closely to see if the hours could be reduced by examining ways and means of improving efficiency.

The company began to make profit from the first three months. Within six months, profit was close to $500,000, or $200,000 in excess of the twelve months target.

Asked what he put the improvement down to, the CEO gave the following reasons:

"Confidence when they quote because they can compare hourly quote rates with TARI®.

"Speed that they get weekly results - Friday after closing books on Wednesday

"Speed that they get monthly results - 4 days instead of 6 weeks."

---

Gross profit can vary from business to business depending on the accounting treatment and when dealing with manufacturing, most accountants will deduct materials plus all factory expenses from sales to derive gross profit.

Theories such as Activity Based Costing- now replaced by Time Based ABC- allocate expenses according to various activities, not just one key activity. So that a process or a product involving more time in setting up the machinery or requiring more of the store man's time in the warehouse will bear a greater proportion of cost.

Given that materials and outsourced work are the most obvious 'direct' cost and that wages tend to be as fixed as the rent in the 21st century, as well as the need to establish a definition of gross profit common to all sectors, TARI® adopts the definition of gross profit of sales less materials as illustrated in Exhibit A.

Neither approach is mutually exclusive for there is ample flexibility for adjustment as required by the specifics of a job, product, or service. The key is to ensure consistency of application.

What reliability can be placed on a small sample of supposedly representative invoices to calculate productivity?

A careful monitoring of a representative sample of 10 invoices across 240 businesses from all sectors, varying in size from $5m to $25 billion, showed the samples reflected an accurate picture to within 1.5% of actual for 97% of the businesses involved and within 5% for the remainder.

This should not come as a surprise bearing in mind the invoice represents a microcosm of the business as whole and a proportion of cost and profit is eventually reflected in every invoice.

CASE STUDY 12:

# BAKER IDENTIFIES WHERE THE RUBBER MEETS THE ROAD

Immersed in baking and distributing 750 products from meat pies to crumpets, it came as a shock when management caught a glimpse of the woods from down in the trees.

The management committee composed of heads of departments sat around the Boardroom table. The CEO had called them together at ten minutes notice to hear what I had to say and it was apparent they resented the short notice.

"I have taken a look at the range of 750 products and I'd like to demonstrate a technique which identifies potential winners and losers and gives a clear message to marketing and production in the process. To start with, perhaps you could give me some idea of what you consider to be your most profitable product?" I asked.

"Crumpets" was the unhesitating and universal response. It was understandable; the winter season was in full swing and crumpets sold well in cold weather. They were a comparatively cheap food to produce, being little more than a light flour mixture pitted with holes and passed over a gas heater at the rate of 12,000 an hour.

"And the next most profitable?" I asked

Answers varied, ranging from meat pies, lemon tarts and sandwich cake, to sausage rolls.

"Well, ignoring the quantities sold for the moment and looking purely at the contribution per man-hour of each product, sausage rolls at $250 per man-hour give the greatest contribution followed by meat pies at $220, crumpets at $77, with sandwich cake as low as $25."

They sat and stared in stunned silence as I wrote the amounts on the whiteboard.

"How did you arrive at that information?" the CEO asked

"The cost accountant had all the information about the hours required to achieve each product as well as the cost of ingredients. It was a matter of getting a simple program written to extract the cost of ingredients, and divide the resulting contribution by the number of hours involved. The result was gross profit contribution per man-hour."

"I'm sorry, but I still don't quite understand"

"Well let's look at meat pies. A pie wholesales at 68 cents and the ingredients cost 18 cents, leaving a gross profit contribution of 50 cents. The plant churns out 10,000 an hour, which makes for a contribution of $5,000 per hour. With 25 staff involved in hands-on production of pies, the contribution works out at $200 per man-hour."

The CEO looked puzzled, "I think I can grasp that, but how could crumpets be so far out seeing they use a lot less labor than meat pies?"

"I agree," said Production who had been experiencing difficulty holding back. "The fact is the contribution on most of the products is much the same based on seventy percent mark-up on factory cost."

"What do you mean by factory cost?" I asked Production

## Baker Identifies Where the Rubber Meets the Road

"Ingredients, direct and indirect labor, supervision, power, depreciation on plant, repairs and maintenance, rent, phones and so on."

"And how do you apportion these costs to the various products?" I asked

"Direct costs such as ingredients, power, and labor go to the product and the rest are spread in proportion to the direct labor. We also apply a small mark up to make a factory profit." He looked around the table before adding "and the factory has never failed to make a profit."

"You say 70% is applied to all factory costs to arrive at the selling price, yet the selling price is pretty well dictated by the market isn't it?" I asked.

"Mostly it is" said the CEO.

The meeting adjourned for lunch during which time we went down to the crumpet line and saw crumpets being packed by hand, as they came off the line.

"They used be machine packed into four a pack, but when we went to six a pack and then eight to meet the competition, we had to use hand labor" said the foreman, "it's slowed us down quite a bit." Production looked stunned.

After lunch, to avoid getting lost in the detail of costing and pricing issues, I suggested we look at the matter from a different angle altogether.

"The sales target for next year is $30,000,000. If we take out $10,000,000 of ingredients and packaging - we are left with $20,000,000 gross profit. You are planning on paying for 220,000 direct labor hours, and you are estimating that 76% of these hours or 166,667 will be productive." I wrote it down on the whiteboard and divided $20,000,000 by 166,667 hours to arrive at $120.

"This means that we need an average gross profit contribution of $120 per hour. We call it target average rate index TARI®, to emphasize it is not a cost but a benchmark. Do we agree?" I looked around the table to see if they were with me.

"I don't see the point" grunted Production, "Where do factory costs, direct and indirect come into that?"

"Excluding ingredients and packaging, all operational costs plus the planned profit are contained in the gross profit of $20,000,000. The $120 is the average contribution per hour based on 76% productivity. "We need to establish a simple program which will track the hours contained in the output as well as the gross profit contribution. We should be in a position to summarize the data weekly and accumulatively and know where we are week to week compared with plan."

"But what about the considerable variation in contribution from product to product that you pointed out?" asked the CEO.

"That's the very point of the exercise" I replied, pleased to have the matter raised by the CEO. "With the TARI® benchmark of $120, we can compare this with the actual contribution from any combination of the 750 active products and see if we can establish a direction for marketing or production or both."

I pointed to the whiteboard where the various contribution rates per hour indicated sausage rolls at $250, meat pies $220, crumpets $77 and sandwich cake $25. "Compared with a benchmark of $120 per hour, what are these figures telling us?" I asked

"Flog sausage rolls and meat pies," said Marketing, sensing a possible lifting of the shackles on pricing, which had held back his marketing initiatives in the past.

"Boost efficiency in crumpets and get out of sandwich cake," said Finance.

Production had difficulty in restraining himself: "If you reckon you can get more efficiency in the crumpet line, good luck to you."

Using an Action Sheet, we agreed on who should do what by when and concluded the meeting.

On a subsequent visit, I learned that Production had resigned to spend more time with his family. It was understandable. Overseeing an output of 750 products a day would drive most to an early retirement.

Finance had taken refuge in computer printouts and Marketing, having won the battle to cull several low selling products, pushed sausage rolls and meat pies and boosted profit to unprecedented levels. The CEO was pleased, but wondered why all this had not been explained before. It seemed so simple.

## Baker Identifies Where the Rubber Meets the Road

An interesting hangover from the traditional management accounting reports surfaced a little further down the track. Based on the new production manager's belief that he could benefit from the available capacity and boost meat pie production with only a marginal increase in power costs, Marketing made a deal to sell meat pies to a supermarket chain at 50 cents, or 18 cents less than the normal wholesale price. One Saturday morning, following a major promotional campaign, 120,000 pies sold and the customers were still screaming for more when an ashen faced production manager decided enough was enough, and threw the switch on a pastry encrusted plant and a dough splattered crew.

After deducting the additional power and ingredient costs, the contribution to the bottom line from the exercise approximated $35,000. Programmed to calculate discounts from the wholesale selling price of 68 cents, the software totaled a discount of $21,600, which in the traditional accounts presentation to the Board of Directors some weeks after the event, indicated that Marketing had, in one hit, used up the budgeted discount for the whole year, leaving an ugly red deficit in the variance column. From that time on, despite earnest attempts from Marketing to explain the profitability of the exercise, there was a strict prohibition on repeating such an exercise. Which viewed philosophically, only serves to highlight the need to get the CEO onside beforehand.

---

Having established a benchmark against which the contribution per hour from each product could be measured, software was developed to extract the contribution per hour per sale – bearing in mind a sale normally included several products. The gross profit contribution flowing from sales was tracked weekly and accumulatively for comparison with plan.

The sales reps were allocated an annual gross profit target broken down into an average gross profit per week and based on achieving an average gross profit percentage per sale of 67% - the percentage relationship between $30m sales and $20m gross profit target.

This business operated state of the art software when it came to taking phone orders. 21 phone receptionists keyed in orders received from school, factory and office canteens, hotels, supermarkets, milk bars, cafes, delicatessens and the like.

The software extracted the ingredients required from each order and accumulated a total ingredient quantity of flour, meat, sugar, butter, eggs, milk and so forth ready for the 7pm arrival of bakers and pastry cooks.

As products streamed off the production lines, they were sorted and matched with orders, allocated into districts and sent for dispatch to waiting delivery vehicles.

Without knowledge of the hours required per product, there was no simple way of identifying the level of productivity at which the plant operated. Had it not been for the conscientious cost accountant hidden away in a small office and neglected by all and sundry as a bygone relic, the information about costs of ingredients, packaging and standard production times would not have been accessible without major expenditure of time and effort.

During one of my visits, a young fresh-faced audit team from a major accounting firm proudly demonstrated that their software gave 96% confidence level of a sample audit check. They also pointed out a hardware box sitting on top of the computer main frame. It was extracting selected data for a Business Intelligence System installed by the consulting arm of their firm as a means of providing management with key information about the business.

Asked if they knew how much waste product was dumped into a huge waste bin and moved out twice a week, they had no idea. Asked what they knew about actual compared with potential capacity of the plant, they shrugged their shoulders. Neither was on their checklist.

Inquiries of the dump truck operator revealed 12 tonnes of waste product was dumped weekly, an amount calculated to be close to $1,000,000 or 5% of total cost of ingredients.

# CASE STUDY 13:

# ARCHITECTURAL PRACTICE ERADICATES MALIGNANT CANCER

A variety of hourly charge rates based on salary levels coupled with dysfunctional time sheets were creating a major distraction until the partners were shown a new way.

Charge rates applied in the Architectural Practice are calculated in much the same way in Accounting, Legal, Consulting Engineering or Surveying and similar professions where hourly rates reflect the various salary levels within the firm.

Smith and Co. operated a two-partner, twelve staff, architectural practice in the heart of the city. The fact that it took only a few minutes to demonstrate their productivity was running at a low-level only exacerbated their discontent with the performance of the practice.

They had gone out of their way to employ a strongly recommended clerical assistant to ensure all time sheets were maintained correctly, but found that it had fallen by the wayside - more due to failure of staff to complete their time sheets than anything else.

Again and again, right in the middle of major design work, they had to down tools and spend valuable time on checking work in progress in order to justify billing clients to get cash in sufficient to cover basic outgoings such as salaries and rent.

There request for help had come in terms of the need to design a better time sheet.

In the first instance, I asked for the paid hours and the target chargeable hours of themselves and their staff with the various hourly charge rates. The chargeable hours were based on the industry average of 65% of paid hours.

### Exhibit A: Ascertaining Potential Gross Fees of Practice

| Name | Planned Chargeable Hours | Hourly Charge Rate $ | Gross Fees |
| --- | --- | --- | --- |
| Partners | 2,800 | 150 | 420,000 |
| Senior A's | 3,200 | 95 | 304,000 |
| Junior A's | 2,600 | 40 | 104,000 |
| Tech. Design | 3,600 | 75 | 270,000 |
| Junior T.D's | 2,600 | 35 | 91,000 |
| Total | 14,800 | 80.34 | 1,189,000 |

Potential Gross Fees = $1,189,000
Actual Gross Fees = $675,000
Productivity % $1,189,000 = 56.8% of planned chargeable hours.

Rather than spend time looking back over somewhat fragmented and unreliable data, we agreed it would be more cost-efficient to plan ahead and track results on a weekly basis. This would provide accurate information as well as highlight problem areas inhibiting progress.

### Exhibit B: Planning & Targeting Performance

| | | |
|---|---|---|
| A | Total expenses | $750,000 |
| B | Target Net Profit | $450,000 |
| C = A + B | Target Revenue (net of disbursements) | $1,200,000 |
| D | Chargeable hours | 14,800 hrs |
| E = C / D | **TARI® (Target Ave Rate Index)** | $81 |
| G = D / 45 wks | Ave weekly hours | 329 hrs |
| H = E x G | Ave weekly billings | $26,649 |
| I = E x G x 45 wks | Check annual billing | $1,199,205 |

I suggested they target an average weekly billing of 330 hours to bring the overall target billings to $1,202,850.

"What does that all mean?" they asked.

"It means that you are tracking an average of 330 hrs by an average of $81 an hour weekly. It means that when you price your work in future, you divide the anticipated fees by a TARI® of $81 to calculate the hours the job should take."

"But what if we use the juniors more than the seniors? The average rate will be much less than $81?"

"It may if you were able to track the individual hours that closely - which hasn't yet been possible despite all your efforts.

"On average, the $81 will be close to the mark. Assume you quote a fee of 10% of a $1,620,000 estimated construction cost. You divide your potential fee of $162,000 by $81 and work out that you need 2,000 hours. You project those hours over the various stages of design and supervision and commence monitoring the job weekly and accumulatively."

### Exhibit C: Example of Job Monitoring
### Week ending: _____

| Job | Target Hrs | Hrs to date | Estimated Hrs to Complete | Variance |
|---|---|---|---|---|
| **XYZ** | 2,000 | 1,200 | 1,000 | - 200 |
| **ABC** | 600 | 400 | 100 | + 100 |
| **Total** | 2,600 | 1,600 | 1,100 | - 100 |

A weekly meeting to review each job captured the hours spent, comparing them accumulatively against the quoted and the estimated time to complete. The meeting served to identify constraints and decide how to overcome them in order to meet target.

It took several weeks of firm but sustained pressure by the partners to get the message across to staff that they needed to be serious about tracking hours, but the process finally grooved in and control over billings was established.

As focus came to bear on the various jobs, hidden benefits emerged, such as discussion of ways and means of reducing hours by varying the design to achieve greater efficiency and still maintain quality. The tone changed from one of laissez-faire or 'she'll be right' to one of 'how can we do this better?'

The annual target net profit was overshot by $75,000.

## Architectural Practice Eradicates Malignant Cancer

Architects are introduced to the methodology relating to charge rates during their university course. In essence, they are taught to work out a charge rate by multiplying the basic wage rate by a factor based on the relationship of wages to total revenue. In essence, a Practice with wages of $400,000 and budgeting for a $1m in revenue would multiply each dollar of wage by 2.5 upwards. It means that a junior on say $30,000 a year would be budgeted to charge out $75,000 or say $50 an hour compared with say $150 for a senior or partner.

This approach is common to legal, accounting, engineering and other like professions and is based on a theoretical assumption the difference in charge rates is due to the level of experience. In other words, the junior charging $50 an hour will take three times as long as the senior charging $150 an hour.

For a client paying the fees, it is of little consequence who did what as long as the job is completed satisfactorily and in line with the quote. It is of no satisfaction to the client to be told a job has gone over quote because a senior had to spend more time than the junior on the job.

Computerized time sheets with associated charge rates make it a very simple matter to print out a list of charge rates on any job at any particular time, providing the times are up-to-date.. In the final analysis, there will be additions and deductions – known as write-offs - due to poor work, incorrect times or failure to input times, which can create major problems of reconciliation.

Thus the need for a benchmark such as TARI® that helps sustain the woods view while down in the trees dealing with the infinite complexities that attend day-to-day events - as demonstrated by an Accounting practice in the following chapter.

## CASE STUDY 14:

# ACCOUNTING FIRM WINS BY LOSING A THIRD OF ITS FEES

Losing a client to a departing staff member is an ever-present concern for professional firms - a problem this practitioner succeeded in overcoming.

When the partners of Jones & Associates reflected on the profession's advertising logo "Not Your Average Accountant," they considered their practice to be well above the average. They practiced out of an upmarket office and ensured the latest magazines were available in a foyer staffed by a chic receptionist to deal with phone and desk inquiries. They also offered regular seminars on matters related to client concerns, including taxation, superannuation, financial planning, computerization, management advice, and general consulting. Actively involved with community clubs, church groups, and other organizations they prided themselves on their marketing outreach.

The only matter that caused them a nagging concern was their end of year profitability, when the time came to split the profit four ways. Each individual share was only half of what partners of the other main practice in town took home. They knew this because of information passed on by the software consultant servicing both practices.

They reviewed their hourly charge rates, which were worked out in the traditional manner by multiplying salaries two and a half times. However, their rates were already higher than the other practice and in their view could not be increased.

They reviewed their productivity, which at an overall 64% of available hours seemed to be in the ballpark for practices of their size.

Then they asked for advice.

"What are your total expenses?" I asked.

"$1,750,000"

"What net profit would you like to see to split between four of you?"

"$150,000 each or $600,000 in total."

"So you are looking for a total gross revenue of $2,350,000. How many hours do you expect to bill for the year ahead?"

"We hope to get at least 64% of paid hours."

Paid hours totaled 37,600 hours. Multiplied by 64% the target billable hours worked out at 23,500hrs, which divided into $2,350,000 to give a nice round average of $100 an hour.

"It seems you are looking for an average of $100 an hour. Based on a 45 week year, that works out at a weekly average of 522 billed hours by $100."

| | |
|---|---|
| **Target billable hours** | **23,500** |
| **No. Weeks** | **45** |
| **Average billable hours per week** | **522 hrs** |
| **Average weekly revenue** | **$522.2 x $100 = $52,220** |
| **Check** | **$52,200 x 45 weeks = $2,349,900** |

## Accounting Firm Wins by Losing a Third of Its Fees

"Our hourly charge rates range from $35 for the junior to $175 for a partner and our timekeeping system is based on different hourly rates for each staff member so we can work out work in progress as well as the cost of a job."

"That will be no problem. When you are about to bill a client, you divide the amount of the bill by the total number of hours spent by various staff members - information available from your software - and work out the average rate achieved. If it is under $100, you may want to review the time taken. If it is over $100, so much the better. Ideally, you will set a target of hours to complete the job before sending the file to a staff member."

"By noon each Thursday, you tally up the hours and rates to be invoiced out by 5pm Friday in order to meet target for the week. You write it up on the whiteboard in the staff room. If you look like being under target, the staff will know what to do, particularly if they are placed on a bonus for every hour billed over target."

"But that means letting the staff know details of practice billings."

"What they don't know they make up. Fear of their full participation would hold back the potential of the practice. The aim should be to harness their undivided input and energy. That is achieved by teamwork with the whole practice focusing on target and cooperating to that end."

"We only bill at the end of each month, and our software system only gives monthly reports."

"Why wait until the end of a month if the job is ready for billing today? Try to bill weekly and apart from improving your cash flow, you can maintain a firm grip on hours and rate if they are monitored week by week."

"What about work in progress. Our hours may be spot on or over the target hours for the week, but can't be billed because jobs are not completed?'

"We are talking about billings only. If you use work in progress hours, you will have discrepancies when it comes to finalizing the account, bearing in mind you write off some of those hours if you feel the client may react adversely. Work in progress hours will tend to even themselves out via the billings. You will find write-offs will gradually fade away altogether as your team becomes focused on targeting what a job should take before it is started."

As often happens, wanting a greater slice of the action, ambitious staff leave for greener fields and despite all contractual agreements, there is an inevitable leakage of clients.

To counter this, the staff were given the opportunity to earn a third of their billings and work largely in their own time, with the proviso that they bill a minimum of 30 hours a week net of any write-offs.

In the next six months, the practice increased its billing by 20% over the same period in the previous year and went on to outdo the targeted net profit per partner.

The nine to five syndrome faded as staff began to enjoy the incentive of one third of their individual charge out rate for every hour billed over their personal 30-hour target in a system where hours over were credited and hours under debited on a three-monthly cycle.

Within a year, the practice became the most profitable of all practices in the four-partner category. It was a pleasure to visit and share in a positive and energizing atmosphere.

---

Software companies have long targeted the public accounting practice as a prime market for practice software and for the potential influence a practice has on its business clients. As a result, systems for time-keeping and charge-out rates have been fine-tuned to a high degree of sophistication. Time is usually costed and based on a minimum of 6-minute units, or 10 units an hour.

While the collation of times and the associated charge rate per client is a simple matter of inputting the client code, the actual billing is frequently subjected to the 'feel' test.

Is the bill too high and should it be written down? Or too low and should be written up? What was it last year? Has the client enjoyed an especially good year?

A practice targeting hours before processing the work, will be in a position to compare target hours with time sheet hours as per the computer printout.

If the practice has adopted TARI®, it will be in a position to compare both time and rate for individual billings.

As most practices rely on monthly feedback from their software, there is seldom any weekly and accumulative comparison of time and rate charged with TARI®.

Reviews, if any, are held two to three weeks into the subsequent month, by which time it is becomes all too difficult to retrieve a poor result.

# CASE STUDY 15:

# LEGAL FIRM TRANSFERS PRODUCTIVITY TO BOTTOM LINE

**U**ncovering a major roadblock to productivity spurred this legal practitioner into clearing the backlog of files strewn across the office floor.

When I first met Bill, he had been running his legal practice for 15 years or so. He said the pressures were unceasing and wondered how he could continue. Every year he told his wife and children the need to work at home nights and weekends would cease and that things would get better. As time passed, he employed additional staff to ease the burden and eventually a partner. However, if anything, pressures increased.

I urged him to make the effort to attend a forthcoming Legal Practice Conference and he promised to try. To my surprise he did attend and I called on him some weeks later. The first thing I noticed was the absence of stacks of files that had previously cluttered the desk and floor of his office.

"What happened?" I asked

"Well, the main thing that hit me was that legal practices with the same staff and partner numbers as mine were bringing in double the fees, some treble. Mine was easily the lowest in fees per staff member. I think they called it 'interfirm comparison'. I could not understand it, since we are so flat-out all the time and charge scale fees for most work and I did not seem to be doing anything noticeably different from the others.

"One of the speakers mentioned a study carried out by IBM, which showed the average typist only typed 8 words a minute during a typical day, due to many interruptions and so forth. It gave me an idea, so when I got back to the office I collected the yellow copies of all work produced in my absence and counted the words typed by the five typists. Would you believe it worked out at 4 words a minute?"

I wondered if he appreciated that he had applied a classic piece of management science to his practice by undertaking an objective measurement of activity. He went with growing excitement,

"I called in Joan, the senior clerk and put it to her that we were typing at the rate of 4 words a minute. She would not have it at all. She said she and the others did at least 65 words a minute. I showed the evidence and pointed out how phone calls, cups of coffee for clients and trips down the street for this and that, eroded the time available for typing.

"I went out and purchased two Dictaphones, one each for my partner and me and five transcribers, one for each typist. I dictated my letters from then on and handed them to Joan who organized the staff. They certainly didn't like the idea of being glued into earphones all day and took days off on sickies, banged doors loudly, stopped making tea and coffee, and generally made life difficult.

"In fact it got so bad, my partner rang me late one evening and asked me to put everything back the way it had been because he couldn't stand it any longer. I agreed, and would have done so, but for an emergency court case that came up and I forgot all about the office for a few days. Suddenly, it all seemed to come together and the staff settled in to the new regime."

He leaned over the desk as though to emphasize the point: "Would you believe that I'm getting my letters back for signing on the same day that I dictated them?"

Waving an arm around to indicate a desk and floor now clear of files, he said, "I used to keep all the current files around me so as not to lose track."

"You mean you were unable to retrieve files easily?" I asked.

"No, it wasn't retrieval so much as keeping in touch with matters dictated which would come back to me for signing anything up to two weeks later. If I kept the file in the office, I would know it was waiting for a typed letter or note."

"What do you intend to do now to make sure it doesn't slip back?" I queried

"I'm going to look at improving the accounts to see if we can do interim billing instead of waiting until matters have reached a conclusion, many months later." He spoke as a man with renewed energy, new life and a motivation to grasp it. His enthusiasm was infectious.

"You know Bill, you didn't have to wait for fifteen years and an almost failed family life and business to go with it." I said.

"Well if someone had told me about 8 words a minute fifteen years ago, I guess I wouldn't have gone through all the pain."

"I'm not referring to the 8 words a minute, helpful though that has been. I'm referring to setting up a clear target of what you need to achieve to cover outgoings including a reasonable take home salary plus some profit."

"I can only do my best."

"Well let's look ahead and see if we can pinpoint what that 'best' represents in terms of profit to two partners."

"Happily" he agreed.

"First step is run through the expenses." Referring to previous statements, we wrote down every item according to Bill's estimates for the year ahead. The total came to $400,000.

"What would you like to make to cover partner salaries and profit for blood, sweat, tears, and risk?" I asked.

"A bit more than last year?" he said tentatively.

"A lot more if you consider the increased productivity you have released. If you only achieve an extra ten hours a day from your five staff, think what that means over twelve months at an average of $70 an hour." With the help of a calculator, I showed him how $70 by ten by five days by 45 weeks added up to an additional $157,500. "I believe you can do better than that." I explained.

We targeted $300,000 profit or $150,000 for each partner, which with expenses amounted to gross fees of $700,000

Looking at the resources available to achieve these fees, the two partners and five staff were targeted average chargeable time of 1,400 hours each, making a total of 9,800 hours, which we rounded off to 10,000 hours.

"You have 10,000 hours to achieve $700,000. Based on a 45 week year that works out at an average of 222 hours a week at a target average rate index, or TARI®, of $70 an hour."

"The hourly rate of $70 seems to be about what we are getting on scale fees," he said.

"The difference now will be the level of productivity. Right now we need to establish a simple feedback system to capture your billings on a week by week basis."

"But as I said, we usually send out our bills at the end of each month, and some matters can't really be billed until they are finished. In addition, we do not always use hours to work the fees out. We use the fee scales indicated by the Law Society."

"It would help your liquidity to bill where possible at the end of each week rather than wait for the end of the month. As for tracking the hours when using scale fees, this can be done by dividing the billing by $70 to calculate what accountants call standard hours."

"But what about work in progress - surely that represent hours of input."

"Yes it does, but you can't pay bills with work in progress."

I showed him a weekly performance summary sheet that would enable him to track results against target each week and accumulatively.

"Is this a sort of interfirm thing?" he asked

"No Bill. This has to do with achieving the potential of this business, given its expense structure and partner take-home expectations. It could well be the resulting average gross fee per staff member is comparable with the average for the profession, but bear in mind the interfirm data is a statistic of a collection of firms operating in a variety of locations and with a varying mix of work.

"The target of $700,000 represents a first cut as it were. As the weekly information feeds back, the picture will become clearer, and enable a second or third cut to be made. Meanwhile, you need to track weekly and accumulatively along the following lines."

### Exhibit A: Summary of Billings week ending: _____

| Invoice No. and Date | Fees<br>A | Number of hours*<br>B | Ave. per hour<br>C = A / B | Disbursements |
|---|---|---|---|---|
|  |  |  |  |  |
|  |  |  |  |  |
|  |  |  |  |  |
|  |  |  |  |  |
| Total |  |  |  |  |
| Total to date |  |  |  |  |
| Target to date |  |  |  |  |
| Variance +/- |  |  |  |  |

* If the hours have not been tracked, then the fees are divided by TARI® to provide calculated or 'standard' hours.

I wrote out an Action Sheet, and we pinpointed who was to do what and by when.

> Many legal practices develop their charge rates based on partner time only - a practice more suited to scale fees per matter.
>
> Charge out rates, calculated and applied in similar fashion to accountants and architects, would quickly drive managing partners into the trees where they tend to get lost in the detail. Thus, the need for a sustained view of the woods, such as TARI® provides.
>
> Even if time sheets are not kept, fees divided by TARI® will provide an overview of 'standard' hours, which if accumulated by the week, will very quickly pinpoint the level of chargeable hours compared with available hours.
>
> Once the backstay of fees in many legal practices, conveyancing has been subjected to fierce competition, putting practices under financial pressure, so the need for targeting and tracking revenue has become a growing imperative for profitable survival.
>
> Noting the likely time a matter will absorb and multiplying by TARI® will provide an estimate of the likely fee. Comparison of the estimate with the final fee will focus attention where the rubber meets the road.
>
> As the following real-life case illustrates, the effectiveness of such an approach is not limited to the professions.

## CASE STUDY 16:

# CONTRACTOR INCREASES STRIKE RATE TO 1 IN 4

A multinational air-conditioning group teaches its contractors across the world how to quote to win installations. This contractor quoted differently.

Two-day seminars had been conducted in five States for a total of 120 installation contractors tied to a multinational manufacturer of commercial and domestic air-conditioning units.

The seminars were directed to improving management skills related to finance, systems, marketing, staff motivation and training.

One exercise involved quoting anonymously for the installation of a commercial unit costing the contractor $3,000 and requiring an estimated six man-hours to install.

Using the method generally in use, which was to mark-up the cost of the unit by 33%, 119 of the 120 contractors quoted between $3,800 and $4,300.

The 120th contractor quoted $3,432, which was so different that I asked whoever it was to explain how he arrived at such a low rate compared with his colleagues.

A tall sun tanned contractor in his mid thirties stood up, "I owe it to my accountant" he said, "I used to mark up like all the others and I was winning about one in every fifteen quotes. One day he suggested I work with an average hourly rate as a benchmark, the same as he did. He called it the TARI® approach or something like that. In this case where no special problems were involved, I merely used the average rate."

"How did you work out the hourly rate?" I was thrilled to find news of an accountant 'out there' who had grasped the concept.

"We worked out what my expenses were likely to be for the year and added a good profit to it. We divided the total by the hours I thought I would be charging out for the same period."

"And what did that come to?" I asked.

"$72" he replied. "That's why my quote came in at $432 plus the cost of the unit. Six hours by $72 were based on two to inspect and quote, four to install."

"Has it made a difference to your strike rate in quoting?"

"Yes, I now win one in four, and I'm well ahead of target for the year." he smiled broadly as he sat down.

I asked him how he kept track of hours charged out. "The accountant gets me to put the hours on the copies of each invoice with the cost of the material, and I drop them into him once a week. He works out how I am going against target and keeps me in touch.

"You don't keep the records yourself then?"

"I started to, but fell behind until I lost track. He keeps me up to it."

# Contractor Increases Strike Rate to 1 in 4

I was asked to address a meeting of the plumbing industry, some of whom are also engaged in installing air conditioning as well as all manner of pipe laying, and so forth. There were about 270 in attendance. Handing out blank sheets of paper, I asked them to write out a quote on a job for which the materials and parts cost $2,000 with an estimated labor time of 10 hours. The quotes were collected and summarized during the coffee break.

When they had settled back in their seats, I asked those with an hourly rate exceeding $50 an hour to indicate by raising their hands. No hand was raised and there was general laughter as though I must be dreaming to think they had an hourly that high.

I then asked for those with an hourly rate exceeding $40 an hour to raise their hands. More laughter and no hands raised.

At rates exceeding $30 an hour a few did raise their hands.

At rates exceeding $20 an hour hands went up everywhere.

"Well you would be interested to know the average hourly rate for the 130 quotes handed in was $65"

There was stunned silence. All of the quotes without exception marked up the materials with an average of 20%, making $400 contribution. If we divide that by the 10 hours we get an additional contribution of $40 an hour. When this is added to what you call your hourly charge-out rate, which averages $25, you can see how the result works out to $65."

I wrote up on the whiteboard:

| Quote Price $ | Cost of Materials $ | Gross Profit $ | Hours | Ave GP per Hour $ |
|---|---|---|---|---|
| 2,650 | 2,000 | 650 | 10 | 65 |

Why, I wondered as I left the venue that day, have we allowed ourselves to be so deluded to the point we can no longer see the woods for the trees.

## CASE STUDY 17:

# HOT BREAD BAKER DISCOVERS MORE TO BREAD THAN FLOUR

Until he came face-to-face with the added value in bread and sausage rolls, the proprietor was actively seeking additional products to boost the bottom line.

Accompanied by his wife, he came in looking a little tired and weary. It was late afternoon and he had been up since pre-dawn in his bakery. A residue of flour whitened his eyebrows and clung to the back of his arms.

"I came to see what you reckoned about my idea of hire-purchasing a pie making machine." he kicked off the conversation. "I can get one that makes 4000 pies an hour and they reckon I can flog them to a wholesaler for 70 cents each. Make a fortune. What do you reckon?"

"Who is 'they'?" I asked, knowing 70 cents was above the price paid by retailers let alone wholesalers.

"The machine people" he fired back. "They should know, being in the business an' all that."

"Well before going into that, do you think we could spend a moment looking at what you do right now?" I steered away from a prolonged and futile debate.

"How many do you employ?" I asked.

"Me and an apprentice pastry cook in the back, and the wife and a part-time assistant in the shop."

"How many loaves of bread would you make in an hour?" I queried.

"110" he said without hesitation.

"And what do sell a loaf for?"

"$1.60"

"And how much would the ingredients cost?"

"24 cents"

I deducted the 24 cents from $1.60 and multiplied 110 by $1.36. "That works out at $150 gross profit an hour or $75 per man-hour if we include the apprentice".

"What about bread rolls, how many of those do you make in an hour?"

"666" he said without a second's thought, "and they sell for 30 cents and the ingredients cost 4 cents."

I multiplied 26 cents by 666.

"That works out at $173 gross per hour, or $86.50 per man-hour. What about sausage rolls?"

"600 an hour selling for 90 cents and ingredients 10 cents," his response came like shots from a gun.

"That works out at $480 gross an hour or $240 per man-hour," I said multiplying 600 by 80 cents. The accountant, who had been observing quietly to this point, permitted a faint smile to crease his features.

"Ah but it's the lamingtons that are my best bet!' The baker exclaimed. "I've got a wholesaler who'll take all the lamingtons I can make." His eyes lit up at the thought.

"How many do you make?" I asked

# Hot Bread Baker Discovers More to Bread than Flour

He had to stop and discuss that with his wife who was sitting placidly beside him.

"Two hundred and fifty an hour," he said, "selling for 65 cents retail and 25 cents wholesale. Material content 8 cents."

"How many would you sell retail compared with wholesale?" I asked.

"Probably three quarters wholesale and a quarter retail".

I quickly calculated the outcome.

"If you sold the full 250 output wholesale it works out at approximately $42.50 or $21.25 contribution per man-hour; and if you sold the lot retail it works out at $142.50 or $71.75 per man-hour."

He looked dumbfounded until he remembered something: "Ah but I've got plans for a machine that will make them a lot faster!"

It was time to plan ahead. Given the fragmentary data available, there was little point carrying the analysis any further.

We reviewed the expenses of the total bakery and excluding materials such as flour and cake mix and arrived at a guesstimated $125,000. His profit the previous year amounted to $25,000. However, given the obvious potential, he was inspired to project a bottom line of $100,000, making a target gross profit of $225,000.

Given a total availability of 4,500 hours in the bakery, and his belief that 75% of those hours would be productive, we targeted 3,250 hours for the planned period, amounting to a TARI® of $69.23 or close to $70 per man-hour.

**Total expenses excluding ingredients**    $125,000
**Target net profit**    $100,000
**Target gross profit**    $225,000

**Target baking hours (75% x 4,500)**    3,250 hrs

**Target average rate index = TARI® =** $\dfrac{\$22{,}5000}{3{,}250 \text{ hrs}}$

     = $69.23 say $70 per hr.

Comparison of $70 an hour with the hourly rates derived from the analysis, suggested that productivity was well below 75%.

Responsibilities were agreed to and recorded on the Action Sheet. The baker agreed to keep a daily record of the product baked, numbers sold and fax the results each week to the accountant who would enter the data and fax back a comparison with target. A meeting was scheduled in four weeks to review progress and make any necessary adjustments to the plan including the TARI® of $70 per hour.

Knowing the baker would have difficulty in designing an appropriate format to record production and sales, the accountant agreed to prepare the sheet and deliver it the following day.

---

It is doubtful if more than one baker in ten thousand has a clear picture of contribution per hour of baking input. As a result, it becomes largely a matter of bakers' instinct as to additional products taken on or rejected.

In this case study, the baker was selling output at retail price in the shop front. Had he been selling at wholesale prices, the gross profit contribution per hour would have been much less.

It was a simple matter to draft a matrix for daily input that would focus attention on where the rubber met the road in his business.

**Summary of Products Baked.**
**Day ............ Week ending ............**

| Product | Sale Price | Ingredients | Gross Profit | Hours | Ave per hour |
|---|---|---|---|---|---|
| Bread 1 | | | | | |
| Bread 2 | | | | | |
| Bread 7 | | | | | |
| Rolls 1 | | | | | |

| | | | | | |
|---|---|---|---|---|---|
| Rolls 2 | | | | | |
| Cakes 1 | | | | | |
| Cakes 2 | | | | | |
| Cakes 6 | | | | | |
| Other | | | | | |
| **Total** | | | | | |
| **Week to date** | | | | | |
| **Weeks to date** | | | | | |
| **Target** | | | | | $70 |
| **Variance +/-** | | | | | |

His problem would be implementation, and everything would be dependent on the level of persistence exercised by the accountant in extracting the completed sheets weekly.

The accountant seemed quite confident. "I expect little trouble collecting the data" he smiled, nodding towards an attractive junior staff member, whose bright, smiling personality more than matched her looks.

## CASE STUDY 18:

# WINDOW MANUFACTURER'S FLAWED FOUNDATION

The fabricator putting a window together was the most productive of all on the assembly floor. It was not his fault the method of assembly was inefficient.

Having successfully acquired a patented aluminum extrusion for making windows with structural strength, the company established a new plant complete with factory, production, engineering, fabricating, marketing and distribution staff, and commenced an extensive advertising campaign.

Consultants were commissioned to set up appropriate systems and procedures from the acquisition of raw materials to the installation of finished product in buildings.

Twelve months down the track, orders were few and far between and the marketing team was under scrutiny by the CEO who accepted the product was new, but only to Australia. It had been tried and tested and well accepted overseas. He accepted the lead-time in getting any new product on the market varied, but with the heavy advertising expenditure over the past year coupled with all the promotions that had taken place, it was time to expect a greater flow of orders than they were getting. The CEO did not agree the price tag was too high. That had been well and truly looked at by the finance team.

Introduced to this debate, as a trainee consultant attached to the senior consultant on the job I was given a stopwatch and, as an exercise, was told to method and work study the window making process going on in the plant. It was a means of getting me out of the senior consultant's hair for a week or so.

I was introduced by the foreman to one of the fabricators engaged on a large window project for a major city building. The foreman explained to a dubious looking employee that it was a matter of me getting on-the-job work experience and there was nothing sinister in taking times for each step of the process.

At the rate of one window a day for five days, I was able to gain a fairly accurate assessment of times and method, as well as becoming very friendly with the fabricator. At the end of five days, I went to the drawing office to set up a scaled down representation on the basis of one quarter inch on the board to represent 36 inches in the plant. I hammered in 2-inch nails to represent the two trestles on which the window lengths had been placed and riveted with their inlays and end pieces. Another nail was hammered in to represent the washroom location and another for the extrusion rack where the lengths were placed each day for fabrication.

Taking a ball of string, I began tracing the pathway of the fabricator as he picked up a length of extrusion, placing it on the trestles, riveting it to a crosspiece, walking down to the other end and repeating the process; and dropping tools occasionally for a visit to the washroom. The ball of string ran out and I tied the end onto a new ball. Two balls ran out and I sent down the road for additional balls until the string went over the nail heads and longer nails were required. Finally after twelve balls of string representing 5 miles weaved backwards and forwards over 6 inch nails, I concluded the exercise. The result looked like a thousand spiders had gone berserk and built a huge pyramid on the drawing board.

The senior consultant was not amused. "You must have added the five days of window making together. You should have averaged the times!" I assured him the times and method had been averaged to represent one window.

Word got around and the factory manager came to look at this phenomenon displayed in the drawing office. When he saw it, he shrugged his shoulders and walked off without a word. He parked his car in the factory corner and walked past the assembly process every day but saw nothing untoward.

The fabricator who worked on the window was astounded that he walked 5 miles a day and wondered if that was the cause of his varicose vein problem. He became very vocal about the extensive length of string tracking visits to and from the washroom.

The finance and marketing directors on their three weekly visits to the plant made a point of checking out this piece of research that they had heard about. The finance director studied it carefully and looked puzzled, whilst the marketing director began to get excited:

"I'd like one of these made up for each of my reps," he said.

"Why so?" asked the finance director.

"Well, when people see what goes into making these windows, they'll understand why it takes so long and costs so much!"

Challenged by the whole exercise, I spent time working out a pre-assembly method which cut the distance down to half a mile and the time to one third.

To me it was a revelation. Here was a big business embarking on a major campaign at no small expense, and yet at the very foundation was a serious flaw that was already threatening survival. Everybody saw it but nobody really saw it. It was all too familiar.

In retrospect, it seemed extraordinary that no one had checked with the European counterparts to find out how they put their windows together, or even how long the fabrication of various configurations should take.

Had they done so, it would have been possible to establish a benchmark for targeting productivity, together with a target gross profit dollar contribution as a focus for meaningful management decision-making.

> Both the factory and production managers parked their cars in a corner of the factory and walked past the window fabrication every day. They saw it but did not see it as it really was.
>
> The senior consultant of the consulting firm with whom I was employed, was up to his eyeballs working with the production manager scheduling purchases and calculating logistics for a nationwide push of the product. He did not see it.
>
> The finance and IT departments were busy preparing a more updated accounts package to cope with the expected demand and the thought never occurred to them.
>
> The marketing department, whose enthusiasm had been somewhat dented by production delays on large buildings, was head down and tail-up working up a long-term promotional strategy for tackling the small home market which they hoped would develop sales in non-structural aluminum windows.
>
> With everybody focused on their part of the ship, there was no one but the CEO at home on the bridge relying on input from his management team to steer the ship into deep waters.
>
> Had I known then about TARI® and invoice sampling to identify productivity, it would only have taken a matter of minutes to illustrate the flaws in the foundation of the new manufacturing and distribution structure under erection.
>
> Even so, it is unlikely the impact on decision-makers would have been anywhere as dramatic as 6-inch nails covered with the equivalent of 5 miles of string.

## CASE STUDY 19:

# MULTI-HOME CONTRACTOR DISCOVERS A NEW WAY HOME

**F**rom the design to the completed house, all looked good on paper, but slippage was occurring. Figuring a way to make the supervisors more accountable turned the situation around.

"I sold and built 75 homes last year, all selected from one of our designs, all subcontracted out to the trades, and in theory, giving me a 10% margin. At an average of $13,300 for each home, I should have made a million to cover office overheads and profit."

"What did you make?" I asked from the other side of a very large teak desk.

"Nowhere near enough to keep the bank off my back. The account is a quarter of a million worse off than this time last year."

"Do you have much owing to you?"

"Receivables are about level with payables." he sighed.

"Are you paying more for your materials and subcontractors than you planned?"

"The estimator reckons we are on track, but I don't know whether he can keep up with it. I mean he's got all his quantities and prices on tap, and orders the materials to site and so on, but the accounts do not always identify what went where, and everything is put into the one bucket. He complains that he does not get informed about what is happening on-site , and in any case, we are always pressing him for a quote for a potential buyer. We might win one out of five quotes. It's pretty tough competition out there."

"How many additional houses could you have built if you had won more quotes?"

"Any number. It's a matter of employing another one or more supervisors."

"How many houses can a supervisor handle?" I asked

"That depends on the design, local terrain, and location. Some are way out of town and take half a day traveling to get there and back. I'd say ours are pretty flat-out handling fifteen a year each."

It was a scenario where phones rang ceaselessly, subcontractors had to be kept busy or be unavailable when required, the right materials had to be on site on time, work coordinated to meet scheduled council inspections or be held up. Pre-designed plans needed to be adjusted to meet varying ground levels and soils in different locations, progress payments had to be attended to and discontented customers to be placated, often requiring adjustments of plan - despite the most comprehensively prepared contracts - leading to additional unpaid work. Things had got out of control.

"Let's look ahead and quantify where we'd like to be in a year's time and then decide how we are going to get there." I reached for a blank sheet of paper.

"We'll list the overheads you have mentioned and guesstimate any increases or decreases in the expenses that have to be met to keep the office open and the business functioning at its current level."

The projected overhead expenses of $750,000 included salaries for five supervisors, the estimator, accountant, receptionist, and two clerical assistants supporting the estimator, the accountant and two sales reps.

When I asked him for input about a desirable net profit, he shrugged his shoulders: "Anybody's guess," and dubiously agreed to my suggested net profit of $250,000, giving a planned gross profit of $1,000,000.

| | |
|---|---|
| **Total Expenses** | $750,000 |
| **Net Profit** | $250,000 |
| **Gross Profit** | $1,000,000 |

"Normally in tracking progress we would identify the key activity and apply an average gross profit rate, or target average rate index, as we prefer to call it, per unit of that activity," I explained.

"One view of the key activity here could be the number of houses, and assuming the same number as last year, that would mean a TARI® benchmark of $13,333 per house:"

$$\text{TARI}® = \frac{\text{Gross Profit}}{\text{No. Houses}} = \frac{\$1,000,000}{75} = \$13,333$$

"This is pretty much the way you have been looking at it, hoping to get a margin on each house sufficient to cover expenses and profit. The theory is fair enough but its success is dependent on how effectively it is controlled. In this case, control appears to require a close degree of coordination between the salesman, the estimator, the accountant, and the supervisor, which is probably asking for more than the realities of the business allow.

"The other view that we recommend to builders is to identify the supervisors time as the key activity. In this case, five supervisors would have an estimated chargeable time of say 6 hours a day for five days a week for 45 weeks. This amounts to 1,350 hours per supervisor or 6,750 hours for five supervisors. We can work out a TARI® benchmark accordingly:

## Exhibit A: Planning and Targeting Performance

| | | |
|---|---|---|
| A | Total Operational Expenses | $750,000 |
| B | Net profit | $250,000 |
| C = A + B | Gross Profit | $1,000,000 |
| D = 1350 x 5 | Total Chargeable hours | 6,750 hrs |
| E = C / D | **TARI®** | $148 – say $150 |
| F | No. Of weeks | 45 wks |
| G = D / F | Ave Chargeable hrs per week | 150hrs |
| H = E x G | Ave Gross Profit per week | $22,500.00 |
| I = F x H | Check ($22,500 x 45 wks) | $1,012,500 |
| J | Total Houses Planned | 75 houses |
| K = D / J | Ave Chargeable hrs per house | 90 hrs |
| L = K x G | Ave Gross Profit per house (90 hrs x $150) | $13,500.00 |

"Translating this back into plain language and given an estimated 75 houses, it means each supervisor has an average of 90 hours per home to make up the chargeable hours of 1350 hours per supervisor. Working on a $150 per supervisor hour and allowing an average of 90 hours per dwelling, it will be possible to bring the job back under control with the supervisors in charge of delivering the gross profit."

## Multi-Home Contractor Discovers a New Way Home

"I wouldn't have thought we need 90 hours supervision for every house." he said, "I'm surprised to hear it. After all, the sub-trades have been with us long enough to know what we expect. We plan 6 weeks per house and I would expect an average of eight hours supervision a week would be maximum. It's not as though as every house is a new design."

"Do you mean your supervisors are underemployed or could manage to supervise more houses?" I asked.

"Well they always seem to be flat-out so I can't say they are underemployed. I guess I haven't really had time to put my mind to the matter this past year what with the downturn of economy, inflation, bank pressures and so on."

"It could have an effect on your pricing." I pointed out. "If we use their hours as a means of targeting the gross profit per house, then the more hours, the greater the price. A house, which costs you $120,000 for materials and sub trades, would normally attract a gross profit of $12,000 based on a 10% mark up. If we estimated supervision at 90 hours, then we would mark up 90 x $150, or $13,500. If we estimated the hours closer to 50 as you indicated, the mark up would be 50 x $150, or $7,500. The fewer hours required, the more competitive you become."

It was obvious that he had never looked at quoting based on supervisory time; he needed time and some factual data to think it through for himself.

In order to gather relevant data and get a clearer perspective of what was actually going on, he agreed to a simple weekly tracking system which pinpoints the time as well as the dollars spent per house and per supervisor and compares the results with target.

The method proved so effective in gaining control and in winning more quotes, he completed 92 homes in the target year without any increase in staff except for the addition of an assistant estimator. Net profit came in at $340,000.

"Next year" he told me, "We'll do better. I am determined to get the cash flow under control so that we can improve on our purchasing. At present we're paying top rates for materials because we can't pay in thirty days; but at least we know the way and how to get there and that's the main thing."

Under the circumstances, I could only agree.

> At the heart of every business, large or small, lies a key driver of activity. There are many drivers and numerous activities, but there is a key driver fundamental to the others.
>
> In this case, it would be reasonable to presume the key driver relates to the number of homes built, but on second thoughts, we can see the key driver is more connected to the building process rather than the house itself, which is the outcome.
>
> Assigning a gross profit value per hour to the supervisors recognizes they are in the driver's seat and accountable for achieving target. Their hours can be tracked and compared with TARI® in conjunction with the overall gross profit achieved on a weekly and accumulative basis.
>
> An approach that points 180 degrees away from the textbook, but as the saying goes; the proof of the pudding lies in the outcome achieved.
>
> Targeting in this manner focused the attention of management and supervisor on the value of an hour of supervisor time and what was needed to achieve its full potential.

CASE STUDY 20:

# HAIRDRESSING SALON CUTS ITS WAY OUT OF CLOSEDOWN

The national award 'Hairdresser of the Year' came at a time when the salon was in danger of closure. By chance, it was selected by a Reality TV Series seeking to film the impact of TARI®.

Since having to pay wages by using their own credit cards, the two partners had been deliberating when they should tell 16 staff and numerous loyal customers that they had no alternative but to close the doors.

Struggling to keep the business alive after the 9/11 collapse of the American tourist trade, they had moved to a more fashionable location. The new salon had a basement for shampoo and head massage, a ground floor for cutting, a first floor for coloring and a second floor for beautician treatment. However, the rent was double that of the previous location.

Anthony, the hairdressing partner, winner of the Hairdresser of the Year Award, attracted top staff and celebrity customers, including models, television and radio stars, senior executives and leading socialites.

No-one looking at the business from outside would have thought that it was experiencing financial difficulties, or that David, the partner in charge of administration, kept up his long-haul flight attendant's role in order to provide cash input from his salary.

It was through a chance meeting with one of their customers, that I met the partners and accepted their invitation to run a health check over the salon.

A twenty-minute on the spot analysis revealed the salon was charging out an average of $81 per hour for a daily average of 3 hrs 51 mins per hairdresser:

**Exhibit A: Estimating Productivity using a representative sample of sales**

| Cash Register No | Sale price net of Tax A | Cost of Materials B | Gross Profit C = A - B | Hours D | Ave GP Per hour E = C / D |
|---|---|---|---|---|---|
| 132 | 160 | 20 | 140 | 2 | 70 |
| 141 | 90 | 20 | 70 | 1.5 | 47 |
| 159 | 145 | 15 | 130 | 1.3 | 104 |
| 180 | 127 | 7 | 120 | 1 | 120 |
| 186 | 215 | 25 | 190 | 2 | 95 |
| 198 | 80 | 15 | 65 | 1 | 65 |
| Total | 817 | 102 | 715 | 8.8 | 81 |

# Hairdressing Salon Cuts Its Way Out of Closedown

| | | |
|---|---|---|
| **Salon Sales** | | $800,000 |
| **Less Materials used & sold** | | $100,000 |
| **Gross profit** | | $700,000 |
| | | |
| **Estimated hours sold: $700,000** = | | 8,641 hours |
| **Ave GP per hour:** $81 | | |
| | | |
| **Hours paid** | | 18,002 hours |
| | | |
| **Productivity %** | 8,641 = | 48% |
| | 18,002 | |
| **48% of an 8-hr day** | = | 3hrs 51 mins. |

Bearing in mind the hairdressers were paid for close to 8 hours a day, the news came as a shock to both Anthony and David, who were under the impression that if anything, they were understaffed and unable to make appointments for potential clients at the busy times.

Times for appointments were reviewed and the hour allocated to a cut was reduced to 45 mins. Some staff objected strongly, claiming it would not be possible to maintain the high level of service if they had to speed up a cut. However, further investigation revealed the one-hour appointment for a cut included a 15-minute shampoo and head massage treatment undertaken by an apprentice. The hairdresser was in fact waiting for the customer at an empty chair during this time. Moreover, the actual cut was completed in 45 mins.

Allowance was made for the initial massage and shampoo by booking the appointment for the hairdresser 15 minutes subsequent to the customer's arrival. Additionally, aspiring models were informed that their discounts of 50% would be cut back to 25%

Targeting expenses plus a reasonable profit, including wages for the two partners for the year ahead, resulted in a TARI® of $99, based on 200 hrs for the week, or 5 hrs 43 min per hairdresser per 8-hour day

Tracking daily and weekly performance for comparison with TARI®, David and the senior staff with whom he shared the results, developed an increasingly clear focus on where the rubber met the road.

Taking advantage of Saturday morning staff meetings prior to opening the doors for the day Action Sheets were introduced, pinpointing who was to do what by when. The staff entered into the exercise with growing enthusiasm, particularly when they saw their ideas for achieving added value through improved service were taken seriously and acted upon.

Action included the nomination of one of the senior hairdressers to monitor progress on customer service, which included more meaningful pre-qualification at the time of booking the appointment. Greater emphasis was placed on s welcoming, and friendly support making use of existing facilities such as tea, coffee, champagne or beer for refreshment and three online computer screens for the computer literate.

The theme came through loud and clear 'We Care.'

Results after the initial 4 weeks revealed the salon was achieving an average of $108 by 4.5 hrs a day per hairdresser. A substantial improvement over a TARI® of $99, although falling below the 5.7 hrs target.

Feeling he was finally getting a grip on the business and that a great burden was slowly but surely lifting from his shoulders, David caught a fresh enthusiasm. No longer wanting to escape from a depressing financial environment, he applied for and received approval from his airline to take 4 months long service leave.

Results after eight weeks revealed the salon was achieving an average hourly rate of $119 with an average output of 5 hrs a day.

For the first time since 9/11, the salon made an operational profit for the month, enough to pay wages to the partners and make inroads into the credit card debt.

Results after 12 weeks, showed an operational profit of $17,100 with an average hourly rate of $127. Productivity however was still below target.

"I used to walk around the salon and chat with staff and customers" said David, "but I became so worried about the finances and the possibility of closing the doors, I shut myself in the office away from it all. It was too painful to do anything else. Now I can see

## Hairdressing Salon Cuts Its Way Out of Closedown

where we are going. TARI® gives me focus and the Action Sheets give me the means of making things happen. We used to take minutes at staff meetings and nothing ever happened. I asked our accountant years ago for input on how to improve the business. He only ever said 'make more money.' Which when you come to think of it was the way to go. At least now we know how."

> This business was using popular salon software to record and track appointments and times per staff member along with payments in and out. They relied on their external accountant for the typical accounts information necessary for compilation of tax returns and annual filing of accounts.
>
> Hourly rates varied from $350 down to $50 and there was a fair degree of discounting especially for actual or potential celebrities.
>
> While there was an awareness of the time a haircut, shampoo or a color would take, there was no follow-through to relate those times with actual times taken by staff.
>
> The salon would appear to be busy all day and all week, but without a means of comparing scheduled or standard times per appointment against actual times, it was not possible to overcome the problem, the symptom of which was manifesting in falling cash levels.
>
> Once the level of productivity was made known and a TARI® established, it became a simple matter of daily and weekly tracking against target to get the salon back on course.
>
> David said the Action Sheet gave him the means of making things happen. Before wrapping up the Case Studies chosen for this book, we will look more closely at the Action Sheet as a means of making things happen.
>
> *A 25 min DVD about the turnaround in this business was filmed in 2006 as part of a TV series "Show Me The Money".*

# CASE STUDY 21:

# MULTI-DEPARTMENT STORE WHITEWASHES THE PAST

It was hammered home that genius was 20% but implementation was 80% of the exercise. This assignment demonstrated a tried and tested technique that made things happen.

It was my first assignment as a fully-fledged consultant and I was determined to do my best. The client company was a major retailer in the city and had been for the past hundred years. They operated a city store and three suburban stores employing 64 buyers for the same number of departments staffed by 2,000 employees.

Sales were based on comparing the sales dollars and number of customers with the same day in the previous year and adding at least the equivalent of inflation. Sales dollars were climbing in the inflationary climate that prevailed, but unit volume had been falling steadily and in absence of any report on unit numbers, the matter had continued unnoticed.

My assignment, originally sold by an engineering-oriented senior consultant, to improve goods flow through the store, changed direction to tackle the unit decline.

I was given an office next to the patriarch MD on the fifth floor - a freshly painted 19th century washroom with a walnut desk and swivel chair sensitively located. The building was old and lifts stopped at the fourth floor, encouraging a fair degree of exercise as I moved up and down to meet with buyers and work on developing new budgets.

Under pain of serious malformation by my consulting supervisor if I omitted a formal Action Meeting each week with the MD and the team of general managers, I complied reluctantly, for it seemed that action was always on me.

### Exhibit A: Action Sheet (shortened for illustration)
Date _____

| No | Item | Action | By Whom | By When |
|----|------|--------|---------|---------|
| 1 | Budgets | Complete Menswear, Kitchenware & Haberdashery | K. C. | (Date) |
|  |  |  |  |  |

**Present: J.J., G.J., B.J., L.J., K.C., Next meeting _____ (date)_____**

After four weeks had passed and I had worked with 34 departments with 30 to go, the supervising consultant - who visited once a week and chatted with the management, told me the client was dissatisfied with progress. They were paying top dollar to the consulting firm, and expected to see more for their money. Overriding my protests that I was flat-out, he said I needed to do something to

## Multi-Department Store Whitewashes the Past

make them feel they were getting their money's worth while I was still working on the budgets.

I looked around to see what could be done and noticed that all the delivery trucks drove off the main street into a lane under the store to drop goods off, and out into another street behind the store. The lane, known as the Receiving Goods Lane was black with the carbon exhaust, dust and dirt of the past hundred years.

At the next action meeting, I brought the matter up by noting Receiving Goods Lane under Item in the Action Sheet.

### Exhibit B: Action Sheet (shortened for illustration)
### Date _____

| No | Item | Action | By Whom | By When |
|----|------|--------|---------|---------|
| 1 | Budgets | Complete Children's Wear, Gift and Food Hall | K. C. | (Date) |
| 2 | Receiving Lane | | | |

After we had dealt with budgets and nominated the departments to be reviewed during the subsequent week, the MD eyed the Lane item with raised eyebrows.

"I put it on the agenda in order to suggest that it be whitewashed. I believe it would make a big difference to the place to have the Lane spruced up". I said as confidently as possible under the circumstances.

There was a long loud silence as I could hear them thinking: '$3,000 a day and he wants to whitewash the Lane'.

The MD sighed audibly and looked over his glasses at the Director of Store Maintenance:

"Will you attend to that George?"

George looked up from his doodling, a little taken aback, "Yes alright Dad" he said.

"When will you do it George?" I asked writing his initials in the By Whom column and poised for the date.

"Oh, next week I suppose." He said watching me inscribe the date accordingly.

After the budgets were dealt with at the subsequent meeting a week later, the matter of whitewashing the Lane arose. It had not been done. All those present knew it hadn't been done, including George, who was hoping it would go away.

"When will you do it George?" I asked with pen poised ready to enter the date.

"Oh, next week. Yes, next week" said George.

When the matter was raised again the following week, nothing had been done. The MD beamed a steely eye at George.

"When will you do it George?" I asked. His father appeared unusually ruffled and I noted the pressure mounting on George as well as his fellow directors. It was about then that I came to appreciate the value of the Action Sheet.

At the next meeting, the budgets were dealt with as usual. The whitewashing of the Lane seemed to stand out more than ever, for we all knew it remained untouched by human hand and George was conspicuous by his absence.

He had been in the firm for 42 years and had successfully withstood many an onslaught knowing that in the face of quiet inaction, things invariably faded after three days or so. However, the Lane would not go away and he was at a loss in how to handle it.

Saturday morning, the MD arrived in his chauffeur-driven Rolls Royce. He did not usually come to work on a Saturday. On this occasion, the Rolls glided into the Lane and stopped. The chauffeur opened the door and assisted the MD into a pair of white overalls before opening the boot to extract two very large pots of whitewash and two large brushes.

Store executives appeared from everywhere and I discreetly withdrew to the sound of George crying "Dad! Dad! For goodness sake!"

On Monday morning, the Lane was almost blinding in its whiteness, an extraordinary transformation from its previous state. Employees heading into the Lane on their way to the security

## Multi-Department Store Whitewashes the Past

entrance were shocked, many thinking they had entered the wrong lane.

For several days I could sense a change of attitude towards me from all the staff, as though they now appreciated I was really worth the money my firm was charging. This was especially so when the General Manager called all the buyers together and informed them I enjoyed the complete confidence of the Board.

For me, it was a revealing insight into the power of the Action Sheet, and I began to use it freely. There were 10 controllers in charge of the 64 buyers and I began action meetings with them weekly, getting agreement on who was going to do what by when.

I encouraged the buyers to have fortnightly meetings with their departments and send me copies of the Action Sheets. However, it was not until the staff at grass roots level realized they could put items on the agenda for discussion and action that they too began to appreciate the value of the exercise.

In nine months, the company turned the corner and began to pick up on unit volume as we monitored numbers of sales and the average sale in each department as a team working together to achieve the desired target. The Action Sheets provided a vital channel through which communication was maintained and action brought to pass.

While awareness of the need to tackle the falling unit volume was vital to the exercise, implementing the changes necessary to bring it about was the key to success.

Two years later, I bumped into James the National Promotions Manager in a busy street not far from the store. "How's it going James?" I asked.

"Fantastic!" he exclaimed in his happy-go-lucky way, "fantastic!"

"What do you put the success down to?" I queried.

"No question, no question, at all!" He said pumping my hand. "Those little sheets you put us onto...what were they called...Action Sheets. Yes that's it, Action Sheets."

He took off as I called out "Are you still keeping them?"

"No need" he yelled above the noise of passing traffic, "everything's alright now!"

Although this case study preceded the development of the TARI® concept, to the extent that it pitched at increasing the number and value of sales it was heading in the right direction.

Important as TARI® is to any business, it is unlikely to groove into the daily routine without a systematic approach to its implementation.

Of all the tools available to management, the Action Sheet has to be rated high on the list. Without it, all the good ideas for improving performance will fall down for lack of a means of implementation.

**Six aspects of the Action Sheet worth noting:**

- Consensus – the person nominated for the action must be at the meeting and in agreement
- Discussion on any item is limited to 5 minutes at most. For example, an item such as 'falling sales' can be dealt with by asking for a report laying out the relevant facts. This approach helps the meeting focus on the first step and avoids the stress of trying to resolve problems at the meeting. Forges a clearer focus on the issues involved. For example, "Bank complaining about slow repayments" may have more to do with collecting accounts receivable, so a discussion about the bank manager could be well off-track.
- Calls for action on 'everybody at the meeting' pinpoints nobody in particular and is unlikely to achieve the desired result.
- Items are numbered according to date, so when they are carried forward it becomes evident how long they have remained on the agenda.
- Meetings chaired by a senior manager will not necessarily achieve the desired input from less senior staff. Better to get the staff to conduct the meetings among themselves once the system has been bedded down, with occasional visits by senior management
- Staff wishing to place items on the agenda need to be able to do so without fear of repercussion. A neutral staff member should be nominated as a recipient for items.

# COMMENTS BY MANAGERS

The following excerpts are taken from comments by senior managers undertaking an MBA program* in Kiev and Odessa, Ukraine, 2006. All are in senior management roles in their companies and have been exposed to Oracle, SAP and other Western oriented software.

\* IBR MBA was graded 'best' among the 140 MBA programs that have been accredited by the Foundation of International Business Administration Accreditation (FIBAA) in 2005 based on the number of excellent grades. The Financial Management segment with its significant emphasis on TARI® concepts was designed and directed by Dr. Keith Cleland. Out of 86 quality criteria in the FIBAA accreditation, 44 percent fell into the category excellent for the IBR MBA. The second best business school, which offers its Executive MBA in collaboration with Kellogg Business School in Germany received only 32 percent in the category excellent.

**A…: Fin Director of a major consulting group who based his assignments on a wholesale and retail chain with $12billion in sales and 70,000 employees.**

"Movement of profitability analysis to the invoice level basis provides management with on-line tools for benchmarking and productivity control. Combined with appropriate IT solution, it lets management identify wrong as well as outstanding performance at the moment of an activity happening."

### A...: Senior Manager with Microsoft

"My recommendation is that the existing reporting system could be more informative if mechanism of TARI® benchmarking was used widely in all reporting information.

Direct link between price, overheads, and productivity is evident from invoice analysis that confirms previous recommendations that the company can boost its productivity and gain profit.

The real help for my company connected with the assignment is that now I try to build a new system of control in my department using internal benchmarking method mentioned above."

### O...: Internet Service Provider

"In the event, invoice analysis proved very helpful to decide which of the company sales are more profitable. In addition, it gives great input for managerial decision-making.. Such analysis

also provides a determinative input for creating a sales plan with more specific indicators for sales department. It makes it possible to focus sales department to a particular kind of sales to reach given objectives.

After this course, I decided to redesign the whole sales process to more closely aligned with the objectives of the company. Such redesign will be dedicated also to the reports, which sales create for management."

### I...: CEO Engineering Division of Plastic Building and Heating Products)

"I was staggered by the first part of the work, when comparing two invoices of a large object and a private house, I got a result, that wholesale is better than retail - that it makes more profit even at considerable discounts on the volume of sales.

The work showed how far my working activity in the company is not effective. Many things which were earlier considered useless (such as monthly and a week reports) became clearer to me in their purposeful use."

### I...: Multinational Building Products

"The assignment demonstrating the use of invoice analysis and the necessity of those figures and the ways of their usage in the managers' work has opened my eyes."

### M...: Multinational Cosmetic distribution

"I am working as a Finance and Administration manager. This module was devoted to the part of finance I thought I know best of all. However, this module opened my eyes to the other sides of cost accounting.

From my everyday business life, the TARI® subject of the managerial accounting is my favorite. It is very interesting to be able to see how a seemingly small decision can influence the total performance of big companies."

### V...: Vice President of a major Port on the Black Sea

"Working out my assignment, I have learned the key to successful implementation of any plan lies in getting relevant and timely feedback to help management's decision-making. Management accounting system should provide substantial information for planning, control, and performance measurement.

Manual analysis of the invoices helped me to understand the structure of the price and cost and how costs are allocated.

I think that my findings could be helpful for my company. I intend to prepare presentation for the top management of my company to communicate my views on cost and management accounting system and how TARI® could be used to improve the efficiency and effectiveness of the Port's existing operations.

And finally, I have recognized clearly that Productivity is key driver for performance improvement."

**O...: GM of Resort Hotel in Ukraine**

"For me working on the Course on "Management and Cost Accounting" proved to be a very exciting and – if I may say so - entertaining experience after dealing with rather scholastic and academic courses on financial accounting and financial planning. The Course on Management Accounting with focus on TARI® seems to give more room for developing creative approaches towards decision-making. In my perception the studying material for the course is closely linked to strategic management, business planning and marketing analysis in the sense that it equips the manager with some essential knowledge in terms of seeking for relevant information needed for controlling the operations, choosing adequate targets and formulating the tasks to the staff as well as making adequate managerial decisions."

---

**Yuri ...: Manager of the Ukrainian branch of a European Group, manufacturing windows.**

"One of the most interesting and new applications was the introduction to TARI® techniques. As a result, a benchmarking standpoint was defined, against which it would be possible to measure the profitability of a certain customer against the 'influx of benefits' in his direction, in future activity. This approach was completely new also in view of the current methodology habitual for the Group of calculating the so-called net contribution based on 'add-on' way to raw materials via transformation costs, ., all the way to the end price formation.

Previously, the management recommended us to estimate net contribution as the process of addition of all the costs and correlating it to the prices effectively applied to this or that customer, i.e. in every profile meter sold for say, 2€ there would be 1€ in raw material, 0.3€ in 'transformation costs' (the process of obtaining the finished product from the 'bulk' of raw materials in production, 0.4€ in the so-called cost-to-serve, an analogue of the sales and delivery costs parameter), and so on. At the end of the day we would arrive at some kind of net contribution related to the price, and it may be positive or negative, but this would not be an approach to treat specific performance against a benchmark; it would be a pure cost-related comparison, with the only possible decision for the management to cut costs wherever possible on a 'big' scale, and maybe overlooking the root of the issue.

"With the current TARI® approach it is possible to see the difference in the contribution of each customer, the time and efforts invested in each, and arrive at a situation when we would be able to assess and create an 'ideal' customer. For instance, Customer B is #3 biggest account, but his prices can be low or we are giving too much commercial incentives to him, also wasting too much time, that as the result we arrive at a 0.69€ rate which is almost half of what we actually want to achieve, according to the calculations. At the same time, we don't invest that much in a small Customer D, though devoting our time to him, and as the result we get a quite optimistic 1.28€ rate.

"The overall importance of this course on financial management lies in the necessity of the financial planning exercises for the local management in order to have a better idea of the company's strong and weak spots, and for appraisal of the ways to market given the current resources and the market situation. The further use of TARI® applications will be of great value not only while planning the internal extrusion activities of our company, but also for sales managers making advice to our customers – the fabricators who feel the acute need to improve performance in their workshops and increase productivity within the framework of their existing assets, to an ever greater degree."

---

**Dr Andreas Kelling, Principal IBR School of Executive Management, Steinbeis University Berlin.**
"Dear Keith,

I met Katia. Cordial greetings from her. She became a fanatic of your teaching now too. She is enthusiastic about TARI® and will introduce this now to XYZ Company, a European company where she is now working as a business development manager. For me her comments were quite interesting: it is like a "depot" effect that your course has. Sometimes, it takes time until people run into dead-ends and need help. In these situations, they remember what you have taught and change their minds. I thought you might rejoice."

## Dr I...: Head of Department sourcing TV programs from Russia and Europe and marketing to subscribers primarily in eastern Ukraine

"In general, we could see on practical example how the TARI® approach could give strong support to the financial management of the company.

Personally, due to this study course and the whole study module I have a possibility to learn in systemic way very important approach to financial management as a basis for successful development and implementation of changes proposals.

The biggest surprise for me was to understand that formal knowledge of mathematics does not guarantee good understanding of finances."

## Y...: Sales Director, Cigarette Manufacturing & Distribution Company

"Monitoring average gross profit per item will be a valuable tool for sales managers allowing them to identify problematic regions/customers. It can also be an instrument of measuring performance of sales force.

This analysis conducted on a regular basis should help the company to achieve improvement of portfolio mix.

I also recommend carrying out invoice analysis (calculating average gross profit per item) on regular basis through automated process in the accounting system. This analysis should serve as a basis for improving portfolio mix.

Personally, I must say that the TARI® concepts add much both to my theoretical knowledge and to practical approach.

Evaluating company's gross profit, not in total, but on product basis is, from my point of view, a key to success. As a sales director, I traditionally concentrated efforts of my team on hitting volume target; but in reality gross profit is much more important."

---

# COMMENTS BY ACCOUNTANTS

**John Bennetts CPA, Gold Coast, Queensland, Australia.**
"Through the urging of a client, we were invited to a presentation by Dr Keith Cleland. At his presentation Dr Cleland spoke about the concept of TARI®. The concept struck a chord and as a result we decided to use this simple tool in the practice.

Our results using TARI® have already improved the average hourly rate from $98 to $135. It is so simple yet has had such a profound impact. Every fee we raise and quote we prepare now has a TARI® of $135 per hour. The most relevant aspect is we have been successful with every quote and have not had one query on our fees.

There is however one negative. I have asked myself why I didn't use this technique years ago. Approximately 17 years ago Dr Cleland spent two days with me assessing my practice and discussed the concept. I didn't implement it because I thought I knew better. How wrong I was. That one decision has cost a fortune.

Thank you Dr Cleland."

---

**Paul M Cooper, CPA, Brisbane, Australia**
"I can certainly see there would be some doubters in believing that a simple management of a few key indicators can cause a major turnaround in business, but as I have mentioned to

you, this has been achieved in the past and is a daily part of my practice... There are many cases I can relate which range from corner stores to workshops making elevators and coal train wagons all of which are thriving on the simple aspects of TARI®."

### D.E. Harris, FCPA, Harris Boscia P/L, Melbourne, Australia

"I wonder how we ever coped before TARI® became available...it has been a boon to our practice".

### Michael Williams FCPA, Balcam Williams, Melbourne, Australia

"As you know we have been using TARI® for the benefit of clients for close on three years now. The simple but powerful concepts underlying this approach to management accounting contributes to a deeper comprehension of the key factors affecting the bottom line. For example, one of our clients had traded for many years but never met the profit expectations of its owners... TARI® helped us analyze the company business into its separate components...and with their focus fixed directly on the key factor in each department, noticeable improvement occurred, with profitability in the year exceeding budget by 50%... The bank is so delighted with the turnaround that it last week approved a new facility of $1m for expansion."

### Richard Vincent, FCA, Robert M.C. Brown Vincent Partners, Sydney, Australia

"I am delighted to provide you with evidence of the benefits obtained and to strongly endorse TARI®. A good example of the benefits flowing is shown through two retailers with three shops each turning over about $4 million and when we took over, each losing between $50,000 and $150,000 a year. Following a split in the family, two shops were taken over by one part of the family and the remaining shop held by the other part of the family. While we remained as accountants for both, only the family holding the single shop adopted TARI®. Within two years that shop produced a profit of $200,000 per annum and has continued to increase. The other two shops continued to experience losses of up to $100,000 per annum. The difference in results was largely due to the information generated through TARI®. Definitely a win-win situation."

### Tom Moon, FCA, T.W. Moon & Company, Sydney, Australia

"As you are aware, I have been involved with TARI® for a period of approximately two years and have had some outstanding successes using the TARI® philosophy and its accompanying software."

### Connor Warin Chartered Accountants, Waltham Abbey UK

"After a successful year, thanks to the TARI® process, we are targeting much higher levels of revenues and profits from our existing business. In addition, we are now providing the new TARI® advisory service to our clients who will generate new revenue streams and fulfilling work for our employees."

### Mike Broderick, Chartered Accountant, York UK.

"We started running a manufacturing client in January last year, and got the hourly recovery from just over £28 to an average of £32.60 for the year. In this year, to date (29 Aug.), the recovery is £37.96 and productivity has improved from 63.8% last year to a remarkable 81.82% this year. As a result, there is a very good bottom line and a very happy bank manager. An offshoot is that the Revenue decided that they were not happy with the accounts, but we managed to persuade the Inspector to visit our client, when we were able to run through the monitoring process and the results, which were being achieved. The result was that a potential investigation was immediately cancelled and we were thanked by the Inspector for our efforts in ensuring the tax bill would be increasing!"

## Gary Morcom & Associates, CPA's, Albert Park, Vic., Australia

"A fabricating client had rung up losses of $166,158 the previous financial year and a further loss of $80,000 for the seven months ending January this year. We got him onto the TARI® program and within a matter of weeks, he was into profit. In eight months February through September (with one week to go), he has recorded a net profit of $138,481. As requested, we asked him to give his reasons for the changes and here they are: confidence when he quotes because he can compare the quoted, contribution with his benchmark; speed that he gets weekly results – each Friday after closing on Wednesday; and speed that he gets monthly results – 4 days instead of 6 weeks."

---

## Poole & Partners, Mooloolaba, Queensland, Australia

"When we first suggested to this client that we could help, he made it very plain that as we knew nothing about jewelry, he didn't think we could! However, he agreed to fax back a weekly summary sales, margins and number of transactions from his two cash registers, Some months later, to our complete surprise, he stands up at a client seminar and sings our praises! In response to your request, we asked him for his comments. He said he liked having a yardstick by which to gauge performance on a weekly basis. The information gained has assisted in developing product mix, formulating pricing policy, obtaining feedback on the effectiveness of marketing activities and given him a better understanding of the cycles impacting the business."

---

## W.A. Sexton, Senior Manager, Cairns Office, PWC, Qld., Australia

"The software is simple, flexible, and easy to implement. The reports are concise and focused, which facilitates improved communication between the client and his advisors. The monitoring facilities are ideal in assisting accountants' complete consulting assignment to banks in respect of business reviews or conducting administrations. We have found clients have been confused by traditional financial statements, particularly understanding the relationship between profit and cash flow. Assisting clients understand this very basic relationship has improved relationships with their banks. We are pleased with the results, particularly in the facilitation of closer relationships with our clients."

---

### Jeffrey A Gill, CPA, South Australia

"TARI® has completely changed the way we look at our own business and those of our clients.

Firstly about our clients. As you will be aware about 2/3 of our income is derived from work done for primary producers and we have about 80 business clients ranging from small building contractors to a handful of clients with a turnover greater than $1million.

I originally had reservations as to whether we would be able to apply the concepts, but the results are far greater than our most optimistic expectations. When I decided to use TARI®, I made a commitment to give it a fair go. I used it even though I knew that some of the time would not be recoverable initially and there was pressure to do compliance work. Looking back, that time was very well spent. I now look at all business clients (large or small) with a TARI® outlook. This means that now, a typical client interview would be 20% discussing tax matters and 80% business management issues. Previously the interview would be tax oriented with a few sympathetic mumbles about how the recession is affecting everyone. Now we can do a meaningful diagnosis of the two or three key factors that affect clients' profitability.

Often when these are clarified for a client, they change the way they look at their business. They will then work through their own solutions. Other times we will make two or three suggestions to improve the key indicator performance. Then they will take up the initiative and implement further measures.

I have a client with an agricultural repair business. This business was largely subject to fluctuations in the surrounding farming area. The neighboring tire business was being sold and it would dovetail into his existing business. We did an analysis of both businesses. Then we did planning for both pointing out the target profitability could be increased by nearly 2/3 by improving his activity and contribution indicators in each business. A consolidated planning report was then printed out. He then took these to his bank manager. The bank manager's response was "this is the best budget submission I have received from an accountant." He immediately granted an increase in the overdraft to meet working capital needs and was confident funding for the tire business would be available. The banker commented that he could see how the improved results were built up and could see the increases were credible.

The second client has just been referred by a bank manager. They are butchers who also do contract slaughtering. Using TARI® we have analyzed the shop and the contract slaughtering separately. We have been able to give pricing recommendations for the individual carcass cuts. From not knowing what to do, these clients are now looking at the things that make up their profitability. These are kilograms sold, pricing of individual cuts, carcass yields and relative profitability of different meats. Previously their pricing was very haphazard. As a result of the new focus, the owner is doing more counter work to sell the newer cuts of meat. The person he replaced was very negative to these sales.

With the work done so far, I would expect these people will go from struggling to meet commitments to having a profitable business. They are innovative in their meat cuts and offering good service but it was not being translated into results.

Using TARI® has further improved our own results. We had previously been using a spreadsheet to obtain similar results. I would estimate that this monitoring of our own business has increased profits by at least half. One thing we are finding is that one of the staff may be doing the analysis and some of the planning. Then I will complete it and see the client. The staff member is getting no feedback on the work carried out.. To overcome this we are planning to have weekly meetings to let everyone know the outcomes. This will also help to upgrade everyone's skills. Over time I hope that it will result in suggestions for strategies from everyone and not just people who finalize the work. If the last 8 months are anything to judge by - then I am certainly looking forward to the coming year."

---

**Michael Schultz, Melbourne, Australia**

When it comes to fiscal reporting, what management desires is simplicity and truth.

In my role as a partner in a medium sized firm of Chartered Accountants and as chairman of a Federal Government initiative to review the effectiveness of advice for management decision-making through the major accounting bodies, the research concluded accountants, increasingly pre-occupied with regulatory demands on their time, do not meet the need for simplicity and truth.

As a result of these findings, a major task of this initiative was to identify key concepts and tools, which would assist management in timely and effective analysis, planning and monitoring.

It was therefore indeed refreshing to discover Dr Keith Cleland's TARI® concept stemming from his years of research at the coal face, threshing out the real needs of business and how best to meet them.

It became apparent that TARI® is what management needed, representing as it does to me, one of the most significant breakthroughs in providing timely and relevant feedback for effective decision-making.

In my capacity as the Director of the International Domain of Mentors and Business Coaches International I continue to coach clients using TARI®, having full confidence the concept will produce simple, powerful and profitable outcomes.

Whether they are Micro businesses, SMEs or Corporates, the concept works, and I have great pleasure and indeed count it as a privilege to record my support."

PS. In April 2004, I lay dying on a hospital bed following liver and kidney failure after a quadruple heart by-pass operation. The life support machine had been removed in a last-ditch attempt to get my heart beating of its own accord.

A thousand miles away, Keith woke up in the night to the thumping sound of a beating heart. Knowing I was in hospital, but unaware of the seriousness of my condition, he was inspired to send off an email the words of which, when read at my hospital bed, came through the mist loud and clear. I woke up to the thump of a new heartbeat that has continued beating strongly ever since.

It is exciting to know the TARI® concept expounded in this book will be the source of a similar wake-up call for a business world looking for a new heartbeat.

# ABOUT THE AUTHOR

Dr Keith Cleland's' background includes seagoing, consulting with an international consulting group, full professor and Head of Departments of Accounting and Business Studies at two universities and chairman of private and public companies.

**Currently** professor and Head, Financial Management Department, IBR School of Executive Management Steinbeis University Berlin*

\* "IBR MBA program was graded 'best' among the 220 MBA programs that have been accredited by the European Federation of Industry (FIBAA) in 2005. The Financial Management segment with its significant emphasis on TARI® concepts, was designed and directed by Dr Keith Cleland. Out of 86 quality criteria, IBR MBA received 44 excellent grades. The second best business school (branch of Kellogg Business School in Germany) received 32 excellent grades."

For the past twenty-five years, he has actively consulted with the accounting profession and their business clients, helping identify and provide solutions for underlying business problems, which led to the crystallisation of TARI® software programmed by software guru Trevor Watters, B. Bus, CPA, and currently installed in over 1,000 accounting practices. With or without software, the TARI® concept has been successfully applied in more than 25,000 businesses with turnovers ranging from A$250K to A$12B+.

**Qualifications** include BA, MA, PhD, Dip Ed (Tertiary), FCPA, MACE

**Relevant publications** include:

- **"Contribution Based Activity – the flip side of Activity Based Costing"** CIMA Management Accounting Journal, UK May, 1997 (selected in 1998 by International Federation of Accountants annual Financial Management Accounting Article Award Competition 1998 for Distinguished Contribution to Management Accounting)
- **Corporate Planning,** USQ 1973
- **Pracdev Key Indicator Reports 2006/7,** Auchinlea Publishers, Sydney (10th Edition) Incorporating Key Performance Indicators of 200+ business sectors.
- **Stratacom** – A Strategy for Learning Commerce. Simulated Business Game, for Schools, Colleges and Business .IBM subsidiary SRA, 1978
- **Surgery & Preventative Medicine for SMEs:** a 10 videos series with accompanying manuals. UNE 1985
- **Practician** – Client Diagnostic Software for the Accounting Profession, 1989 with Trevor Watters, B.BUS, CPA., upgraded to Windows as **TARI®** 1999.
- **Client Focused Management** module of the Australian CPA Society's BAS (Business Advisory Services) Series. 1994/5
- **Identifying Key Value Drivers** module in the Management Advisory Series of the Australian Institute of Chartered Accountants. 1994/5
- **Basic Instincts** – Case Study in Contribution Based Activity, Financial Management Journal UK – a CIMA (Chartered Institute of Management Accounting) publication May 2001
- **Driven to Distraction,** Financial Management Journal, UK - a CIMA publication, September 2002

About the Author

- **Limitations of Time Driven Activity Based Costing** from a Contribution Based Activity perspective. Financial Management Journal, UK - a CIMA publication October 2004
- **Balancing the Accounting Scorecard** – accepted by the Academic Roundtable, for presentation at the June 2009 Annual Conference of the IMA (Institute of Management Accountants, USA)

# DEFINITION OF TERMS

**Activity** refers to the key activity fundamental to and driving all other activities. It can be man or machine hours or minutes, number of sales, meals (covers) served, t tons per mile, skins tanned, and so forth.

**Actual v Potential** refers to the actual output of a business compared with potential output, given the available resources of personnel, equipment and technology.

**Added Value** refers to the operational expenses plus profit excluding materials or goods. Same as **Gross Profit**.

**Capacity** refers to the output potential of a business. For example, "At 80% of capacity, the business produces 8000 widgets", meaning that at a 100% capacity, the business is capable of producing 10,000 widgets.

**Chargeable Activity** is the same as **Output Activity**.

**Contribution** refers to **Gross Profit**.

**Efficiency** a business can increase productivity by improving the method, time and back-up involved in carrying out an activity. (Case Study 18 provides a good example).

**Gross Profit** in this book refers to the margin between sales and cost of goods or materials. It is often referred to as 'contribution' or 'added value'. There is no universal agreement on the definition of gross profit. In manufacturing and similar businesses, it is frequently defined as sales less (cost of materials + factory on costs). Can also be defined as (expenses + profit) where expenses and profit refer to operational expenses and profit and exclude cost of goods or materials and outsourced work.

**Invoice** same as **Billing:** refers to the amount charged out to customers. Tax is always excluded when analyzing invoices or billings

**Net Profit** refers to the bottom line after all operational and non-operational income and expenditure is accounted for.

**Oncosts** refers to costs that are added on such as rent, power, depreciation and so forth.

**Output Activity** refers to the units of key activity such as hours, minutes, number of sales, meals (covers), room-nights, charged and invoiced. It is often referred to as 'productive units of activity' as compared with 'available units of activity'.

**Profit** refers to the bottom line or what is left over after all operational income and expenses are accounted for.

**Productivity** refers to output for a given input.

**Rate** is short for the gross profit per unit of output activity

**Revenue:** Sales by another name

**Target Average Rate** refers to the average gross profit per unit of output activity that has been planned as a target benchmark

**Target Average Rate Index - TARI®** - same as Target Average Rate but with Index added to emphasize its status as a benchmark and not a cost to be applied.

**Unit** refers to a single unit of output activity such as a man or machine hour or a minute, a sale, a meal (cover), a ton per mile.

# FAST TRACK PROBLEM RESOLUTION GUIDE

|  | Case Study |
|---|---|
| **Cash drying up?** | 5, 9, 20 |
| **Marketing in need of support?** | 6, 12, 10 |
| **Jobs profitable, net profit poor?** | 2, 11 |
| **Working 'flat-out' and getting nowhere?** | 5, 9, 18 |
| **Starting up a business?** | 7, 8 |
| **Planning for the next period?** | 8, 10 |
| **Check profitability of product or job?** | 1, 2, 10 |
| **Losing out on quotes?** | 4, 10, 16 |
| **Buying - or merging - an existing business?** | 6, 10, 11 |
| **Need to cull some products?** | 3, 12 |
| **Setting charge rates in a professional practice?** | 13, 14, 15 |
| **Establishing an incentive system?** | 4, 14 |
| **Want to get a foot in the door of a big customer?** | 2, 10 |
| **Competition proving strong?** | 3, 10, 16 |
| **Problem with pricing?** | 5, 19, 20 |
| **Looking for more profitable products?** | 10, 12, 17 |
| **Can't get new ideas implemented?** | 21 |
| **Want to check staff productivity?** | 7, 11, 20 |
| **Targeting and achieving Net Profit?** | 2, 7, 8, 9 |
| **Want to improve feedback?** | 7, 11 |
| **Relying on Time Sheets?** | 4, 13 |
| **Difference between Productivity and Efficiency** | 15, 18 |

# EPILOGUE

I loved heading down to the sea in ships that made their way to distant ports of the world trading cargoes of many kinds. Once clear of the noise, smells, pollution, and turmoil of port and out to sea, a smooth and steady rhythm settled upon the ship. Leaving loved ones behind we went about our duties dulled by sweet sorrow until awaking like new beings to the movement of long swell beneath the keel, soaring of albatross on a gentle breeze, luminous stars in a clear sky.

An influence stronger than the sea drew me ashore where like a fish out of water I floundered in a strange and hostile environment. Someone said 'study accounting by correspondence' and that is what I did, working all hours to qualify in record time.

Halfway through my studies, I talked my way onto a branch accountant's job in an insurance office with 13 girls. Until that point an account was what appeared in the study books as a/c. Ignorant of what they looked like, I asked for 'the books' and the senior girl brought them to my desk. After two weeks - by which time I had worked out the connection between the books and the study material - the manager sent for me and said 'Keith, it's you or them, and I can't afford to lose 13 girls, so it looks like you. It seems they don't like working for someone who orders them around like the first mate of a sailing ship." I was astounded, but took note and whispered requests from that time on.

Once qualified as a CPA, in recognition of passing exams in the shortest time of their 100 years in business, the Correspondence

College, asked me to take on the job of State Principal. I quickly accepted and in my enthusiasm for the course, enrolled a record number of students. So much so, the CEO asked me to explain my methods to the other Principals. When they discovered I had nothing to impart about techniques of marketing or salesmanship, but was merely operating out of enthusiasm, their ballooning interest deflated.

Seeking truth, I studied all the subjects in philosophy and political science, qualifying with Bachelor of Arts and a Commonwealth Government prize. Truth still elusive, I signed on for a thesis on the subject of Jean Jacques Rousseau's "Political Obligation and the General Will." On completion of the thesis and getting no closer to truth with an MA in philosophy, I joined an international consulting group hoping at least, to find the truth about big business.

To my considerable surprise, I learned that big business was in essence, small business writ large; being in most cases an amalgam of branches or departments and that success within a business had as much to do with nepotism and politics as competence. Two case studies in the book recount typical experiences.

Finding no ultimate truth in big business, I took time off to go gold mining, achieving a measure of success in finding truth but no gold.

Responding to the call for those with practical as well as academic qualifications, I took on a role as senior lecturer in accounting and business studies in a new type of university offering degrees "similar to but different from" the traditional universities. The "University of Southern Queensland" gained a reputation for graduating 'practically oriented' students and after twelve months, I became Head of School and began to develop contacts with businesses locally and nationally. In those days Corporate Planning was the flavor of the month and we were able to get the attention and active participation of CEOs of major industries in the first Corporate Planning Conference held in the country.

Offered a foundation chair as professor and Head of Department of Accounting and Business Studies in the University of Technology in Papua New Guinea I signed a five-year contract and took off. Once in situ, the position opened up active participation with the United Nations Committee on Small Business development in Asia and the Pacific and I was invited to join the National Economic Advisory Council.

In an attempt to reconcile the significant differences between a Western-driven approach to business development and local cultural attitudes to white man's ways, I worked on and completed a PhD on a strategy for Small Business Development in P.N.G.

The end of contract coincided with the need for our son to attend high school, so we relocated to a research position in a university town back in Australia. The research focused on small-medium enterprises (SMEs) and it was here that I came to see what we were teaching in accounting and finance, had little relevance to the management-decision making needs of business in general, small or large. How best to identify and then resolve those needs were to absorb my time and energy over the next 25 years.

In the process, I came to see that business was as much a part of the mainstream of life as arts, science, sports, or philosophy. It provides food to eat, facilities to communicate, transport for trade and travel, gas, electricity, water, houses and hospitals. It can be likened to a bloodstream, sustaining life, as we know it on this planet, with shortage and starvation arising from natural or man-made blockages.

I saw that failure of a business follows a long period of stress for the owners, managers and families, for staff and their families, for unpaid suppliers and their families, and to a lesser degree, the surrounding community and their families. Moreover, I saw the accumulative effect of many failures influencing the medical, social, economic, and spiritual well-being of a nation. I saw $millions upon $millions raised in the search of cures for cancer, but little research into the malignancy of problems at work in business as a prime source of cancer in the body.

Conversely, I saw the success of a business arrived at by honest endeavor and competent management, does more for the well-being of a nation than any tonic medicine has been able to devise.

TARI® is the author's contribution to the success of business.

# APPENDIX

## The Business Wheel

Two keys form the hub: **output activity** and **contribution**

*Business Wheel diagram with segments: Marketing, Innovation, Finance, Human Resources, Operations, Production; central hub: TARI® = Av. GP Contribution per unit of Output*

**Target Average Rate Index = TARI®**
**(Target Average Gross Profit Contribution per unit of Output Activity)**

**Output activity** refers to physically measurable units of key activity traceable in output, for example, minutes, hours, number of sales, meals, tonnes, kilometres, tins of beans, etc.

Contribution **refers to gross profit (or added value) calculated as sales less cost of goods or materials used.**

## How's Your Wheel?

Lacking awareness or feedback on what really drives the hub; the great majority of Business Wheels remain elliptical resulting in stress on all parts, as evidenced in the assessment of 12 senior managers as they viewed their businesses in wheel format, grading each departmental spoke on a 1-10 grid.

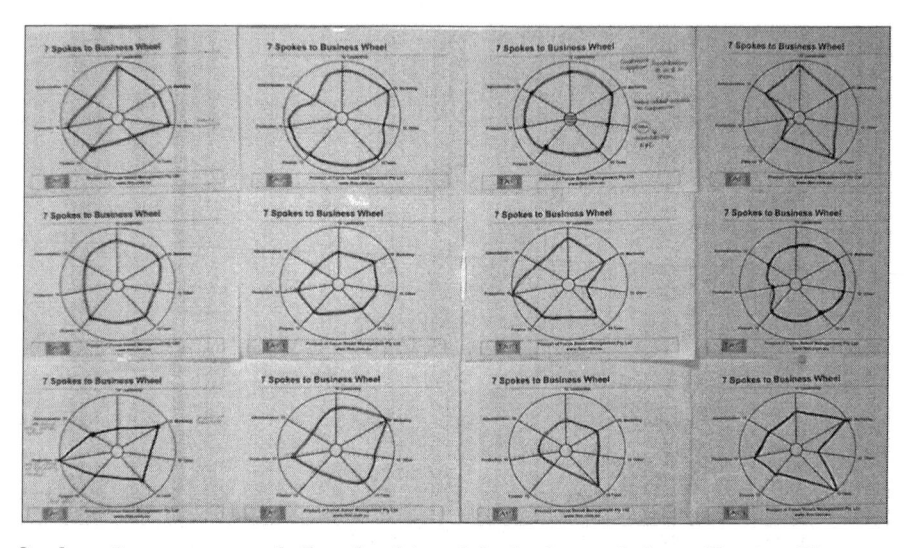

*Spokes from top read Leadership, Marketing, Other, Team, Finance, Production, Administration.*

Printed in Great Britain
by Amazon.co.uk, Ltd.,
Marston Gate.